Cooking Well

Healthy Chinese

Wang Renxiang & David W. Wang
with Jo Brielyn

Cooking Well: Healthy Chinese
Text copyright © 2013 Hatherleigh Press

Hatherleigh Press is committed to preserving and protecting the natural resources of the Earth. Environmentally responsible and sustainable practices are embraced within the company's mission statement.

Hatherleigh Press is a member of the Publishers Earth Alliance, committed to preserving and protecting the natural resources of the planet while developing a sustainable business model for the book publishing industry.

This book was edited and designed in the village of Hobart, New York. Hobart is a community that has embraced books and publishing as a component of its livelihood. There are several unique bookstores in the village. For more information, please visit www.hobartbookvillage.com.

DISCLAIMER
This book offers general cooking and eating suggestions for educational purposes only. In no case should it be a substitute nor replace a healthcare professional. Consult your healthcare professional to determine which foods are safe for you and to establish the right diet for your personal nutritional needs.

Library of Congress Cataloging-in-Publication Data is available upon request.
ISBN 978-1-57826-428-5

All Hatherleigh Press titles are available for bulk purchase, special promotions, and premiums. For information about reselling and special purchase opportunities, please call 1-800-528-2550 and ask for the Special Sales Manager.

Cover and Interior Design by Nick Macagnone

10 9 8 7 6 5 4 3 2 1

Printed in the United States

www.hatherleighpress.com

Table of Contents

CHAPTER 1

The History of Chinese Cuisine

C hina is a country known for its appreciation for the culinary arts and its deliberate use of ingredients. Preparation, balance, and presentation all play important roles in Chinese cuisine. In the Chinese culture cooking has long been viewed not merely as a task or a means to an end, but as an art form all its own. This view of cooking as an art dates as far back as the classical age of China, during the Chou Dynasty in 1122–1249 BC.

Taoism and Confucianism, the two most prevalent philosophies in Chinese culture, both stress the significance of the culinary arts in daily life. Their influence is seen in cooking standards and hygiene, in achieving a harmony of ingredients, in consideration for the healthful attributes of food items, and in the value placed on the taste, appearance, and texture of food.

Confucius taught his followers that proper table etiquette and culinary standards were essential. Many of his teachings regarding food are still practiced in Chinese culture today. One such example of wisdom that is still observed was the idea that using knives at the dinner table was in poor taste. To eliminate the need for knives at the table, cooks were encouraged

1

to chop ingredients into smaller, bite-size pieces during meal preparation. Confucianism also influenced the notion that good cooking was dependent on learning to incorporate a variety of ingredients and seasonings, instead of relying solely on the taste of individual food items. This idea that cooking involved the perfect marriage of items—for visual appeal, texture, and taste— helped to advance Chinese cuisine into an art form.

In contrast to Confucianism's focus on wedding the taste, texture, and appearance of food, Taoism was more concerned with the beneficial, life-sustaining attributes of food. Taoism helped facilitate the development of many hygienic elements in food preparation and cooking in Chinese culture. The basic premise of Taoism regarding cuisine was that food was given to nourish the body and that it should be used as a means of preserving health and promoting longevity. Following the philosophy that the Taoists had developed in 500 BC may very well offer solutions to a variety of diet and health problems faced by today's society.

As with traditional cuisines from most other countries, the basic ingredients for Chinese cooking were dictated by the food items that were available at the time.

Here are a few of the basics, still used in a variety of modern Chinese dishes:

Rice and/or Millet: Rice and millet are two grains that are mainstays of the Chinese diet. Rice has been farmed in China since ancient times. In these areas, rice's place in the meal is comparable with that of bread in the Western palate. In areas in northern China where rice did not grow, millet was farmed instead. Millet is a small, round grain that is often used as an alternative to other grains because of its versatility. A few of the most commonly used forms of rice in Chinese cuisine are:

- *Long-grain rice:* Many Chinese meals are prepared with long-grain rice (brown or white) because it produces fluffier rice. If a recipe calls for long-grain rice and you need to use short- or medium-grain rice instead, reduce the water by 1/4–½ cup per cup of rice to attain that fluffy consistency.
- *Glutinous rice (also known as sticky rice or sweet rice):* In China, sticky rice is used mostly for making snacks and sweets. In many other parts of Asia, however, glutinous rice is often used in place of regular rice. Milled glutinous rice is white and completely opaque. Unmilled glutinous rice contains bran that gives it a purple or black appearance.

- *Rice porridge (congee):* Rice can also be made into rice porridge by adding more water than usual during the cooking stage. The rice becomes saturated with the water and becomes very soft and glue-like. Rice porridge is eaten with bamboo shoots, pickled tofu, pickles, and salted duck eggs, as well as many other condiments.

Noodles: In wheat-farming areas in northern China, people largely rely on flour-based food such as noodles, pancakes, dumplings, and steamed buns. Noodles are another staple food in Chinese cuisine, with a long history and widespread popularity. Long noodles are a symbol of longevity in Chinese tradition. Thus, during birthday celebrations, people will serve "longevity noodles" in wishing for longer life.

Soybeans: The soybean is also indigenous to China and plays an important role in Chinese cuisine. Soybeans are the main ingredient in tofu and are also the source for soy milk and soy sauce. Soybean sprouts are often used in Chinese dishes, as they provide an excellent source of protein while enhancing a dish's flavor.

Vegetables, Fruits, and Herbs: A variety of vegetables, fruits, and herbs have comprised a large portion of Chinese cuisine for centuries. Ingredients such as scallion (green onion), garlic, cucumber, peach, tomato, ginger, cilantro, melon, and apple have been incorporated into the Chinese diet both for their ability to add flavor and for their medicinal merits.

Tea: Often considered the national drink of China, tea has its roots in that region. Drinking tea is included in daily life and accompanies most meals in Chinese culture. Tea finds its way into important Chinese ceremonies and traditions as well.

Did You Know?

- Food has always held a place of prominence in Chinese culture. Food was at the center of festivities and rituals at the imperial court, and continues to be at the heart of all significant celebrations and events, such as births, weddings, deaths, and the Chinese New Year. In fact, out of roughly 4,000 people who were employed at the palace, over 2,200 of those people worked solely on the planning, preparing, caring for, and serving of the imperial meals.

- Fortune cookies are not really Chinese and aren't found in China. They are an American invention.

- Cold drinks like juice and soda aren't typically served with meals in China. Instead, most people have tea or soup with their meals.

- It is believed that the use of chopsticks originated during the Shang Dynasty (over 3,000 years ago) due to the abundance of traditions and superstitions regarding knives and other utensils. For instance, Confucius taught his followers that knives were linked to acts of aggression and didn't belong at the dinner table.

CHAPTER 2

The Staples of Chinese Cuisine and Their Health Benefits

There are a number of misconceptions held by Americans about the ingredients and nutritious content found in Chinese cuisine. This is due largely to the fact that many of the dishes served in "Chinese" restaurants in the United States have been altered and "Americanized" to fit the desires and tastes of our culture. Menus in our restaurants feature a greater number of fattening and meat-based dishes, which is not indicative of traditional Chinese cuisine. Next time you order, skip over the deep-fried items and choose from the vegetarian section of the menu. Stir-fried entrées that include bok choy, broccoli, spinach, or cabbage with a side of white or brown rice provide a more authentic experience and a healthier meal.

A traditional Chinese diet consists mainly of plant-based foods and drinks, including whole grains, legumes, vegetables, fruits, mushrooms, nuts, seeds, and both black and green teas. It also contains only small amounts of fish and poultry, primarily for flavoring. Red meat is consumed very infrequently. In fact, a traditional Chinese diet consists of only around 20 percent animal products—considerably less than the typical American diet. The average person in China amasses between 6 and 24 percent of his or her daily calories from fat, compared to the average American's 39 percent. The daily fiber intake of the average person in China is also three times greater than that of the average American.

Cold dishes play a special role in Chinese cuisine. Often designed to contrast or balance out other dishes, the harmonious blending of textures, colors, and flavors are characteristic of Chinese cuisine. Cold dishes in China are mostly cooked after cutting and seasoning. Different from warm dishes, cold dishes are characterized by extremely fresh ingredients (most often vegetables) and particular emphasis on taste, crispiness, and color.

Incorporating the "Chinese way" of eating into your daily diet is an excellent recipe for a healthier way of life. To begin, fill your plate with mostly complex carbohydrates (like vegetables, rice, and noodles) and employ meat as more of a flavor enhancer than as the centerpiece of your meal.

A balanced Chinese meal contains two key elements. The goal is to reach a harmony of taste, color, aroma, and texture by balancing the principles of "Fan and Tsai."

1. The fan element consists of grains and starches, normally white rice, noodles, or dumplings.

2. The tsai element is the vegetable and meat portion.

In China, people believe that food is a crucial part of staying healthy, preventing and curing diseases, building up a good physique, and prolonging one's life. This traditional relationship in China between food and medicine dates back nearly 5,000 years. The famous Chinese medical book Shen Nong's Pharmacopoeia (Shen Nong Bencao Jing) recorded many medicinal uses of everyday ingredients, such as dates, sesame, yams, grapes, walnuts, lilies, lotus seeds, ginger, and wheat germ. It has developed into a practical science of nutrition over the course of a thousand years. Medicinal food is not just a simple combination of food and traditional medicine. It is a distinctive cuisine following the theory of traditional Chinese medicine, which is made by using both medicine and food as components and processing them through cooking. Many recipes still have important applications today and are applied in daily cooking.

The Yin and Yang Concept of Health

Hot and cold. Yin and yang. The concept lies at the core of Chinese culture, so it only makes sense that it would also play an important role in Chinese cuisine and meal planning. Chinese culture emphasizes the importance of maintaining balance. In cuisine, that applies to having a balance of colors, flavors, and textures in foods. It also extends further. Certain foods are believed to possess cooling (yin) properties and others to have warming (yang) ones. The goal is to consume meals that maintain a healthy balance between the two.

In relation to food, yin is cool, expansive, moistening, light, and upward growing. Yang is warm contractive, drying, compact, and downward growing. Yin foods, such as fruits and vegetables, are cooling to the body and lower the internal thermostat. Animal-based foods are yang foods because they contain concentrated proteins that warm the body.

Examples of yin foods include:
- All fruits and vegetables (excluding seaweed)
- Sugar and sweeter foods
- Alcohol
- Fresh and soft dairy products

Examples of yang foods include:
- Salt and salty foods
- Caviar
- Aged salty cheeses
- Red meat
- Poultry

Some foods are also excellent for calming your blood and clearing heat and toxins from the body. Try these yin foods to clear heat: tomatoes, watermelons, wheat, apples, potatoes, asparagus, bananas, broccoli, cabbage, cantaloupe, cauliflower, celery, cucumbers, dandelions, eggplant, elder flowers, grapefruit, lemons, lettuce, marjoram, millet, pears, and peppermint.

Most Chinese medicinal food is used for the purpose of preventing illness rather than being eaten as a cure. For example, it is believed that soup prepared with carefully chosen ingredients has the power to both prevent and cure diseases, to nourish and rebalance the body, and to boost the immune system. In chapter 4, you will find a selection of recipes featuring traditional medicinal foods.

Here are a few of the basic ingredients found in Chinese cuisine and the benefits they provide:

- **Scallions (or green onions):** Scallions are used mostly for flavoring in Chinese cuisine, but also offer health and medicinal benefits. They help promote digestion and kill oral and respiratory bacteria. Scallions are also used in Chinese culture to relieve congestion and chills and to relax muscle tension. A traditional Chinese medicine used for the early treatment of colds consists of a blend of scallions, brown sugar, and ginger.
- **Chinese vegetables:** Chinese vegetables like broccoli, cabbage, and bok choy are nutrient-dense foods that have high amounts of minerals, vitamins, fiber, and antioxidants.
- **Ginger:** Ginger is a root that is often used to season Chinese cuisine. It also provides a great deal of medicinal relief for ailments. Ginger is used to treat nausea, diarrhea, bloating, headaches, bleeding, colds, coughs, and inflammatory diseases. It also aids in digestion and promotes circulatory and cardiovascular health.
- **Garlic:** Chinese cuisine generally contains large amounts of garlic. In addition to enhancing the flavor of Chinese dishes, garlic helps with digestion, prevents diarrhea, and kills bacteria. Garlic has also been linked to lowering the risks of stomach and colon cancer, and is also used in Chinese culture as a therapy for diabetes, hypertension, and hepatitis.
- **Tofu:** Tofu is a product of soybeans and is a part of many traditional Chinese meals. It is known to help lower total cholesterol levels by as much as 30 percent, lower low-density lipoprotein (LDL, or bad cholesterol) levels by up to 35–40 percent, lower triglyceride levels, and is believed to play a role in raising the levels of high-density lipoprotein (HDL, or good cholesterol). Increased intake of tofu has also been linked to a lower risk of anemia, a deficiency of red blood cells. Tofu has a low calorie count, a relatively large amount of protein, and very little fat. It is also high in iron and calcium. Some studies have found that soy protein is correlated with significant

decreases in serum cholesterol, LDL, and triglyceride concentrations.

Note: You may run into difficulty when trying to locate the more exotic ingredients needed for some Chinese cuisine recipes. Substitutions have been provided throughout the book to help you customize the recipes to your needs and to the availability of the items.

Here are some ingredients commonly used in Chinese cuisine:

- **Chinese cooking wine:** Made from rice, this ingredient is also known as rice cooking wine. It can be found in the seasoning section of most Asian grocery stores or supermarkets. You will likely see both white and dark varieties, which are interchangeable, although the darker variety does have a stronger flavor.
- **Black/white rice vinegar:** There are two basic kinds of vinegar, white or black (dark). Most often, your selection will depend on what color the finished dish will be. White vinegar is typically used in cold dishes and light-color recipes, whereas dark vinegar is more often used in stir-fry and dark-color dishes. Other than coloring, these vinegars are interchangeable.
- **Sweet-flour sauce/paste:** This can be found in the seasoning/sauce section in many Asian grocery stores. A common replacement can be plum sauce.
- **Fermented/preserved black bean:** This ingredient is made by fermenting and salting black soybeans. They are most widely used for making black bean sauce and can be found in many Asian grocery stores.
- **Szechuan chili paste/Szechuan chili broad bean paste:** These two spices are common in Szechuan cooking and both can be found in most Asian grocery stores.
- **White pepper powder:** This spice is different from black pepper powder, as it is more finely ground and tastes milder. It can be found in the spice section of most Asian grocery stores or supermarkets. If you cannot find it, replace with black pepper powder, but use a lesser amount.
- **Szechuan peppercorn, peppercorn powder, and peppercorn oil:** This spice has a unique aroma and flavor that is not hot or pungent like black, white, or chili peppers. Both peppercorn and peppercorn oil are essential ingredients for Szechuan cuisine. It can be found in many Asian grocery stores.
- **Bamboo shoots:** The most common bamboo shoots are winter bamboo shoots (which are larger in size) and spring bamboo shoots. These are sold in various processed shapes and are available in fresh, frozen, dried, and canned

varieties in many Asian grocery stores. (The frozen and canned varieties are easiest to find, but fresh or dried are preferred.) Whenever mentioned in this book, winter and spring bamboo shoots can be used interchangeably.

- **Black wood-ear mushrooms:** Also known as black fungus or tree ears in China, this is an edible fungus used primarily in Asian cuisine. Wood ears are sold mainly in dried form and can be found in many Asian grocery stores. Before using, soak the fungus in warm water for at least fifteen minutes. It will puff up to several times its normal size. Rinse and trim the stem before cutting.

- **Enoki mushrooms:** Enoki, which means "golden needle mushroom" in Chinese, are long, thin white mushrooms used in East Asian cuisine. They are available fresh or canned. A common replacement is oyster mushrooms.

- **Shiitake mushrooms:** These mushrooms are a symbol of longevity in Asia. Due to their health-promoting properties, they have been used medicinally by the Chinese for more than 2,000 years.

- **Straw mushrooms:** Canned straw mushrooms can be easily found in many Asian grocery stores. For the recipes in this book, we recommend only dried varieties. If you cannot find these in your local Asian grocery, they can also be found online.

- **Winter melon:** Also called white gourd, ash gourd, "fuzzy gourd," or "fuzzy melon," this melon is vine grown and prized for its very large fruit. It is typically eaten as a vegetable when matured.

- **Lotus seeds:** Lotus seeds or lotus nuts are the seeds of plants in the genus Nelumbo, particularly the species Nelumbo nucifera. They are most commonly sold in shelled and dried forms.

- **Chinese red dates:** Commonly known as jujubes outside of China, these dates are regarded as both a fruit/spice and an herb. You can find these fresh during the autumn, when they're crisp and green as apples, or dried, when the fruit takes on a deep red color and sweet, chewy texture. Dried red dates can be found in most Asian grocery stores.

- **Chinese pearl barley (coix seed):** This is a widely used ingredient in Chinese cuisine. Barley also soothes the stomach, so it is beneficial if you have an easily irritable stomach.

- **Chinese lettuce (celtuce):** Also known as stem lettuce, celery lettuce, or asparagus lettuce, this is a cultivar of lettuce grown primarily for its thick stem and is used as a vegetable. It is especially popular in China.

- **Seaweed:** Seaweed is used extensively in China, Japan, and Korea for soups or to wrap sushi. You can find this in many Asian grocery stores, most commonly sold as sheets.
- **Shanghai bok choy (Chinese Napa cabbage):** This Chinese leaf vegetable is often used in Chinese cuisine. Baby bok choy (also known as Shanghai bok choy) refers to greener varieties.
- **Chinese broccoli:** This is a leafy vegetable featuring thick, flat, glossy blue-green leaves with thick stems and a small number of tiny flower heads similar to those of broccoli.
- **Szechuan pickled/preserved vegetable:** Known as zha cai in Chinese, this is a type of pickled mustard plant stem originating from Szechuan. It can be found in many Asian grocery stores.

CHAPTER 3

Cooking and Dining Tips

C hinese cooks believe that the aromas and colors of their food dishes are almost as important as the actual taste. The texture and flavors of your ingredients excite the taste buds, while the careful presentation of visually appealing, colorful items provides extra sensory gratification to the recipient of the meal.

Remember to take these qualities into consideration when shopping for, preparing, and serving the Chinese cuisine you create using the recipes in this book. Choose only the crispest, ripest items. To achieve the best taste and reap the highest health benefits from your Chinese dishes, use fresh, ripe vegetables, fruits, spices, and herbs from your garden, local farm stand, or farmer's market whenever possible.

Here are some helpful sources for finding authentic ingredients:

- Many items can be found in the ethnic section of your local supermarkets.

- More exotic ingredients may need to be purchased from Chinatowns or Asian supermarkets in your area.

- If local sources are limited in your area or specific ingredients prove difficult to locate, don't discount the vast resources available to you online. The supply of authentic Chinese ingredients and spices has widened greatly thanks to the Internet and the many online stores at your fingertips.

Whether serving your Chinese cuisine to family members, guests, or simply enjoying it yourself, eating your food with chopsticks will add an authentic touch to the meal. Here are a few pointers to make your experience with chopsticks a success.

Picking Up Food with Chopsticks:
1. Hold the first chopstick between your ring and middle fingers. This chopstick will stay stationary. Use your thumb to help keep it in place.
2. Slide the second chopstick between your thumb and index finger. This chopstick can be controlled by moving the index finger up and down. This will open and close the chopsticks, and will allow you to pick up food.

Eating Rice with Chopsticks:
1. Rice is eaten directly from a bowl. Lift it to your lips.
2. Use the chopsticks to scoop the rice into your mouth.

Here are some DOS and DON'TS to practice when eating with chopsticks:
- DO use your chopsticks to cut food into smaller pieces when necessary. Using chopsticks to cut up the larger pieces of food is acceptable, since you don't have a knife. Simply squeeze the food between your two chopsticks and split it in half.
- DO use bamboo or wooden chopsticks while learning. Chopsticks made from wood or bamboo are easier to use than plastic or metal chopsticks.

Metal and plastic chopsticks are slippery, which can make it more difficult to get a tight grip on the food.
- DO NOT use your chopsticks to point at people or things. It is considered rude in Chinese culture.
- DO NOT pick up your food by stabbing it with your chopsticks. Again, this is considered inappropriate table etiquette.
- DO NOT cross your chopsticks. In Chinese culture, crossed chopsticks are the symbol of death. When chopsticks are placed on the table, they should be parallel to each other.

Quick Tip

Many of the ingredients used to prepare Chinese cuisine burn quickly if they are not watched closely. Also, many of the steps involved in recreating Chinese recipes are for short time periods of 2 minutes or less. It is best to limit the distractions in your kitchen and keep your attention on your cooking when preparing Chinese cuisine to prevent overcooking or burning your meals.

Interesting Facts About Chinese Cuisine

- Most Chinese soups use stock, typically made from chicken bones, pork bones, or beef bones. For the recipes in this book, you can choose to make your own stock or purchase stock from your local grocery store. When using store-bought stock, look for low-sodium, all-natural options as a healthy choice.
- Seafood is very important in the Chinese kitchen. To the Chinese, the freshest seafood is odorless and is best cooked by steaming with a little seasoning to bring out the natural sweetness of the seafood.
- Depending on the amount of water that is extracted from the tofu curds, fresh tofu can be divided into several varieties: Tofu flower (douhua in Chinese), soft/silken tofu, and firm tofu.
  - Tofu flower is a soy-based dessert that has a pudding or custard texture. This sweet treat is generally served with a sweet ginger syrup.

- Soft/silken tofu is undrained tofu that contains the highest moisture content of all fresh tofus. Its texture can be described as similar to that of very fine custard.
- Firm tofu, although drained and pressed, still contains a great amount of moisture. It has the firmness of raw meat but bounces back readily when pressed.

Cooking Methods

Here are a few of the common cooking methods used for preparing Chinese cuisine:

- **Stir-Fry:** Stir-frying is the classic Chinese cooking method. It is usually done over a gas stove, although an electric one can be used. Stir-fry is generally a mixture of meat or seafood, vegetables, and tofu. The ingredients are sliced thin or diced. The meat or seafood is soaked in a marinade of soy sauce, salt, and other seasonings. All the ingredients are cooked together in a wok (a round-bottomed cooking pan). Stir-frying is a fast and easy method.
- **Steaming:** Chinese food is often steamed in bamboo containers that can be stacked one on top of the other. This allows different kinds of foods to be cooked at once, so it saves time and fuel. The most common examples of steamed foods are dim sum, dumplings, and fish.
- **Red Stewing or Red Cooking:** This cooking technique is unique to Chinese cuisine. Food is cooked very slowly over low heat. Generally, meats are browned first and then cooked in water or broth with soy sauce, wine, and seasonings. Tougher cuts of meat may be used in red cooking, since it takes several hours to cook using this method. This type of cooking earned its name from the rich brown sauce it produces.
- **Boiling:** Ingredients (usually vegetables) are washed and cut, and then cooked in boiling water until they are slightly tender. Vegetables are often cooked using this method and served with a sauce. Boiling foods helps preserve their color, texture, shape, and nutritional benefits.

CHAPTER 4

The Recipes

Staple Foods
Rice & Noodles

Basic Fried Rice

Ingredients

1 tablespoon oil
2 eggs, beaten
1 tablespoon chopped green onion (scallions)
4 cups cooked rice
1 tablespoon soy sauce or oyster sauce, as desired
1 teaspoon salt

Directions

1. Heat a wok or frying pan. Add 1 teaspoon of oil, heating until hot. Turn heat down, add eggs, and stir until set, then cut into smaller chunks using a spatula. Remove from the wok and set aside.

2. Add remaining oil to the wok. Add green onion to bring out the fragrance.

3. Add cooked rice. Stir for a few minutes until heated through.

4. Add soy sauce and salt, stirring for a minute.

5. Add egg chunks. Mix thoroughly.

This is a basic recipe for fried rice that can be adjusted as desired. Many meats, vegetables, and spices can be added to this basic recipe to produce variations of all kinds.

The key to making fried rice is using rice that has been previously cooked. Long-grain rice, which comes out fluffier and is less sticky than other varieties, is perfect for fried-rice dishes.

Cooking the egg for fried rice:

There are several ways to do this. Some prefer to fry the beaten egg and cut it into strips to use as a garnish. Others prefer to scramble the egg and mix it in with the rice: the egg is scrambled separately and added to the rice in the final stages of cooking. Either method is fine.

One of the secrets of fried rice is that the ingredients are cooked separately—helping to maintain their distinct flavors—and then combined in the final stages of cooking.

Vegetarian Fried Rice

Ingredients

2 tablespoons green peas (if frozen, thaw first)

1 tablespoon cooking oil

2 eggs, beaten

6 white mushrooms, diced

1 medium onion, diced

½ red bell pepper, diced

1 teaspoon salt, or to taste

4 cups cooked rice (long-grain jasmine rice preferred)

1 tablespoon soy sauce, either light or dark

1 tablespoon green onion (scallions), chopped

Directions

1. Boil water in a saucepan. Add green peas and cook for 1 minute. Drain and set aside.

2. Put 1 teaspoon of oil in the wok and heat until hot. Turn down heat and pour in the beaten eggs. Stir until completely set, and then break into smaller chunks. Remove from the wok and set aside.

3. Put remaining oil in the wok and heat until hot. Turn heat to medium, add mushrooms, and stir for 1 minute.

4. Add onions, green peas, diced red bell pepper, and salt. Stir for 2 minutes.

5. Add cooked rice and soy sauce. Stir for 3 minutes or until heated through.

6. Add egg chunks and toss in chopped green onion. Mix well with vegetables.

Yangzhou Fried Rice

Ingredients

½ cup green peas (if frozen, thaw first)

4 ounces medium-size shrimp, shelled and deveined

1½ tablespoons cooking oil

2 eggs, beaten

1 tablespoon chopped green on-ion (scallions)

2 tablespoons diced carrot

4 Chinese sausages, roast pork, or ham, diced

4 cups precooked rice

3 tablespoons light soy sauce

Salt, to taste

Directions

1. Boil some water in a saucepan. Add green peas to boil for 1–2 minutes. Drain and set aside.

2. Parboil the shrimp; drain and set aside.

3. Put 1 teaspoon of oil in a wok and heat until hot. Lower heat and pour in the beaten egg, stirring until completely set. Remove from the wok and set aside.

4. Add remaining oil in the wok; add chopped green onion and diced carrots. Stir for 1 minute.

5. Add salt and sausage; stir for 2 minutes.

6. Add rice and soy sauce; stir for 2 minutes or until rice individually separates and heats through.

7. Add green peas, shrimp, and egg chunks. Stir for 1 minute and mix everything together.

Yangzhou fried rice, a version of fried rice popular in southeastern China, tastes fresh and delicious, with a soft and savory quality. Also referred to as Yangzhou egg fried rice, this is a simple homemade dish, often made from leftover rice and other dishes. Naturally, there is a great variety of styles of Yangzhou fried rice, among which Fried Rice with Meat and Vegetables is the most well-known.

Fried Rice with Chicken

Ingredients

2 tablespoons cooking oil

2 eggs, beaten

1 cup cabbage, thinly shredded

1 medium onion, diced

½ cup green peas (if frozen, thaw first)

4 cups cooked rice

2 tablespoons light soy sauce

1 teaspoon oyster sauce, or as desired

½ teaspoon salt, or to taste

8 ounces cooked chicken, diced or shredded

Directions

1. Put 1 teaspoon oil in a wok and heat until hot. Turn down heat and pour in the beaten egg, stirring until completely set. Remove from the wok, cut into strips or scramble into chunks, and set aside.

2. Stir-fry the shredded cabbage and diced onion on high heat for 1–2 minutes; remove and set aside. Do the same for the green peas.

3. Add oil. Turn down heat to medium and stir-fry the rice. Add the soy sauce, oyster sauce, and salt.

4. Add chicken, onion, cabbage, and green peas. Stir and mix well.

5. Add egg chunks and mix everything together.

There are several kinds of noodles in Chinese cuisine: egg noodles (or *mein*), rice noodles, and wheat noodles. In the northern regions of China, wheat noodles, more so than rice, are eaten as the staple food. Rice noodles (also known as vermicelli) are more commonly consumed in southern China. The noodles eaten by the Chinese come in varying widths and thickness, and are usually used to symbolize long life to the Chinese. For this reason, noodles are commonly served at birthday celebrations. The main distinction between these two popular dishes is in how the noodles are prepared.

The normal way of treating noodles is to boil them first. When they are then stir-fried with other ingredients, it is called *"chow mein"* in English. The common dry and brittle kind of "chow mein" found in Chinese restaurants in the West is virtually unknown in China. While it can be found in some places in Canton and Hong Kong, it is primarily made for foreigners. In China, chow mein is made with soft noodles.

Shanghai-Style Noodles

Ingredients

6 ounces Shanghai-style noodles
(if not available, substitute with
Japanese udon noodles)
1½ tablespoons cooking oil
2 cups shredded cabbage
1 cup bean sprouts

1 tablespoon green onion
(scallions), chopped
2 tablespoons soy sauce
½ teaspoon salt, or to taste
½ teaspoon sesame oil

Directions

1. In a large saucepan, cook the noodles in boiling water until they are tender, but still firm. Drain and rinse with cold water. Drain again and set aside.
2. Heat cooking oil in wok.
3. Stir-fry cabbage for 4–5 minutes.
4. Add noodles, bean sprouts, and green onion. Stir.
5. Add soy sauce and salt. Stir and mix well.
6. Sprinkle sesame oil.

Shrimp Noodles with Vegetables

Ingredients

4 ounces small- or medium-size
raw shrimp, shelled and deveined
1 teaspoon cornstarch
1 teaspoon rice cooking wine
½ pound Chinese egg noodles
2 tablespoons cooking oil
1 teaspoon minced ginger
½ cup shredded Napa cabbage

1 piece frozen bamboo shoot,
thawed, rinsed, and cut into
shreds (optional)
1 red bell pepper, cut into thin
strips about 2 inches long
1 tablespoon light soy sauce
1 tablespoon oyster sauce
½ teaspoon salt, or to taste
Several drops sesame oil

Directions

1. Marinate raw shrimp with 1 teaspoon of cornstarch and 1 teaspoon of rice cooking wine for 10–15 minutes.

2. In a large saucepan, add water and boil noodles. Stir to separate. Cook until tender but still firm. Drain and rinse with cold water. Drain again and set aside.

3. Heat the wok, adding 1 tablespoon of oil. When the oil is hot, add ginger. Stir for about 20 seconds and add shrimp. Stir until they turn pink. Remove and set aside.

4. Add 1 tablespoon of oil to the wok. Heat until hot, add cabbage and bamboo shreds, and stir for 2 minutes.

5. Add the red bell pepper. Stir-fry for 1 minute.

6. Add noodles, soy sauce, oyster sauce, and salt. Stir and mix well

7. Add shrimp. Mix everything together.

8. Sprinkle sesame oil on top.

(see note on next page)

Bamboo shoots or bamboo sprouts are the edible parts (new bamboo culms that come out of the ground) of many bamboo species. They are used in numerous Asian dishes and broths, and are considered a gift from nature for their unique fresh taste and texture. Bamboo shoots are low in fat and calories, and are a good source of fiber. They are also a good source of potassium, which is a heart-healthy mineral, and help to maintain normal blood pressure and a steady heartbeat. Most common bamboo shoots are winter bamboo shoots (bigger in size) and spring bamboo shoots. They are sold in various processed shapes, and are available in fresh, frozen, dried, and canned versions in many Asian grocery stores. The frozen variations are the easiest to find, while canned ones are always available, but they are not recommended for use. Whenever used in these recipes, winter and spring bamboo shoots are interchangeable.

Chicken Chow Mein

Ingredients

1 boneless, skinless chicken breast (about 7–8 ounces), cut into thin shreds

1 teaspoon cornstarch

⅓ teaspoon salt

1 teaspoon soy sauce

¼ cup water

½ pound Chinese egg noodles

2½ tablespoons cooking oil

1 clove garlic, sliced

1 teaspoon minced ginger

½ pound mung bean sprouts

½ cups shredded cabbages

½ red bell pepper, thinly shredded

1 tablespoon chopped green onion (scallions)

1 tablespoon oyster sauce

¼ cup chicken broth

1 tablespoon soy sauce

½ teaspoon sesame oil

Salt, to taste

Directions

1. Marinate chicken breasts with 1 teaspoon of cornstarch, ⅓ teaspoon of salt, and 1 teaspoon of soy sauce for 15 minutes.

2. In a large saucepan, add enough water and boil noodles. Stir to separate. Cook until tender but still firm. Drain and rinse with cold water. Drain again and set aside.

3. Heat the wok. Add 1 tablespoon of cooking oil. When the oil is heated, add garlic and minced ginger. Stir for 20 seconds to bring out the fragrance.

4. Add marinated chicken shreds. Stir-fry until cooked. Remove and set aside.

5. Add ½ tablespoon oil, heating until hot. Add mung bean sprouts, cabbage, and red pepper shreds. Stir quickly for 1–2 minutes until mung bean sprouts are soft but still crispy. Remove and set aside.

6. Add remaining cooking oil in the wok and heat until hot. Add green onions, salt, soy sauce, oyster sauce, and chicken broth. Add noodles, bean sprouts, red bell pepper, and chicken shreds. Stir until sauces are well-absorbed and well-mixed.

7. Toss in sesame oil.

Spicy Szechuan-Style Noodles

Ingredients

1 tablespoon sesame paste

2 teaspoons sesame oil

3 teaspoons hot chili oil

1 tablespoon black rice vinegar or any vinegar

2 tablespoons light soy sauce

2 teaspoons dark soy sauce

½ teaspoon salt

1 teaspoon Szechuan peppercorn powder

3 teaspoons sugar

2 green onions (scallions), finely chopped

½ cup chicken broth

12 ounces dried Chinese noodles

Directions

1. Combine all ingredients (except noodles) in a bowl. Mix very well.
2. Boil the dried noodles in a large saucepan for 5 minutes or until tender, but still firm. Drain well and place in a large bowl.
3. Stir the sauce mixture into the noodles.
4. Stir and mix well.

An assortment of vegetables, such as mung bean sprouts, snow pea tips (both need to be briefly blanched in boiling water first), or raw shredded cucumber can be used to turn this into a delicious vegetarian main dish.

There are two basic kinds of vinegar, white and black (dark). Most often it depends on what color the finished dish will be. White vinegar is typically used in most cold and light-color dishes, while dark vinegar is more often used in stir-fry or dark-color dishes. Other than in terms of coloring, both vinegars are interchangeable.

Basic Cold Noodles

Ingredients

12 ounces egg noodles, fresh or dry
1 tablespoon cooking oil
2 green onions (scallions), finely chopped
2 teaspoons chili oil (optional)
2 teaspoons sesame oil

2 teaspoons vinegar
1 tablespoon sugar
2 teaspoons light soy sauce
½ teaspoon salt
½ teaspoon white pepper powder or black pepper powder
¼ cup chopped red pepper

Directions

1. Cook noodles in boiling water for 3–5 minutes (depending on whether noodles are fresh or dry). Rinse with cold water until cool. Drain and set aside.
2. Heat 1 tablespoon of cooking oil in wok. Add all ingredients when hot, and stir for 1 minute.
3. Remove from heat and pour over noodles immediately.
4. Serve when noodles are cool.

White pepper powder is one of the important ingredients in Chinese soup cooking, and is always served as the final touch to the soup. White pepper powder, which is different from black pepper powder, is grounded more finely and tastes milder. It can be found in the spice section of most Asian grocery stores or supermarkets. If you cannot find it, replace with black pepper powder, but use a smaller amount.

Cold noodles are often served as a simple main dish in the summer. Various vegetables can be used as a side dish, the most popular of which are mung bean sprouts (boil for 1 minute first, and then let cool), cucumber strips, snow pea tips, spinach, or other green leafy vegetables.

Cold Noodles with Sesame Sauce

Ingredients

12 ounces Chinese egg noodles
1 tablespoon sesame oil
3 tablespoons sesame paste (or peanut butter)
1 tablespoon hot water
1½ tablespoons light soy sauce

1 tablespoon vinegar
¼ teaspoon salt, or to taste
2 teaspoons sugar
1 tablespoon cooking oil
2 green onions (scallions), finely chopped

Directions

1. Cook the noodles in boiling water until tender but still firm. Gently stir and separate strands during boiling. Rinse under cold running water. Drain well. Place in a large bowl and toss with sesame oil to prevent sticking.

2. In a small bowl, mix the sesame paste with hot water, and blend together well. Then add sesame oil, soy sauce, vinegar, salt, and sugar. Mix everything together well.

3. Heat wok until hot. Add 1 tablespoon of cooking oil and chopped green onion. Stir for 20 seconds.

4. Pour hot oil directly into the seasoning bowl, mixing everything well.

5. Pour sauce mixture over noodles. Mix to coat well, serving cold.

If you like spicy flavor, use some hot chili oil (to taste). If you can't find sesame paste, use peanut butter instead.

Stir-Fried Rice Noodles with Pork and Oyster Sauce

Ingredients

5 ounces fresh lean pork
1 tablespoon soy sauce
½ teaspoon cornstarch
1 teaspoon rice cooking wine
1¼ teaspoons salt, or to taste
5 dried Chinese mushrooms

12 ounces rice noodle (vermicelli)
2½ tablespoons cooking oil
½ onion, cut into thin shreds
2 cups mung bean sprouts
3 tablespoons oyster sauce

Directions

1. Marinate pork with 1 teaspoon of soy sauce, ½ teaspoon of cornstarch, 1 teaspoon of rice cooking wine, and ¼ teaspoon of salt. Cut into shreds.
2. Soak mushrooms in warm water for 40 minutes or until soft. Cut into shreds.
3. Boil vermicelli until loosened. Rinse with cold water, drain, and set aside.
4. Heat 1 tablespoon of oil in wok and stir in shredded pork until color changes. Add onion and mushrooms, and stir until everything is cooked. Set aside.
5. Heat remaining oil in wok again. Add vermicelli, stir for 1 minute, and then add mung bean sprouts, stirring to heat through. Add pork, onion, mushrooms, oyster sauce, soy sauce, and salt. Stir to mix everything well.

Vermicelli is a clear rice noodle. You can find it in most Asian supermarkets, and it comes in many varieties.

Stir-Fried Noodles with Assorted Meats

Ingredients

¼ pound lean pork, thinly shredded

2 teaspoons and 1 teaspoon cornstarch

2 tablespoons soy sauce

1 teaspoon salt, or to taste

25 small-medium sized shrimps, shelled, deveined

¼ pound chicken breast, thinly shredded

1 teaspoon rice wine

5 dried Chinese mushrooms

10 ounces Chinese noodle

3 tablespoons cooking oil

1 clove garlic, minced

1 teaspoon minced ginger

1 cup bamboo shoots, shredded

½ cup ham, shredded

1 cup snow peas, parboiled

1 tablespoon oyster sauce

1 tablespoon green onion (scallions), chopped

¼ teaspoon white-pepper powder or black-pepper powder

Directions

1. Marinate pork in mixture consisting of 1 teaspoon of cornstarch, 1 teaspoon of soy sauce, and ¼ teaspoon of salt for 15 minutes.

2. Marinate chicken breast in mixture consisting of 1 teaspoon of cornstarch, 1 teaspoon of soy sauce, and ¼ teaspoon of salt for 15 minutes.

3. Marinate shrimp in mixture consisting of 1 teaspoon of rice wine, 1 teaspoon of cornstarch, and a pinch of salt for 15 minutes.

4. Soak mushrooms in warm water for 30 minutes or until softened, then cut them into shreds.

5. Boil noodles in water for 3–5 minutes (do not overcook). Drain and rinse under cold running water. Drain again and set aside.

6. Heat the wok over medium-high heat. Add 1½ tablespoons of oil; when hot, add garlic and ginger (to bring out the fragrance), then stir in the pork and chicken.

7. When color turns, add shrimp, mushroom, bamboo shoots, ham, and snow peas. Stir for 2–3 minutes. Remove and set aside.

8. Add remaining oil in the wok and heat until hot. Add noodles, soy sauce, oyster sauce, and salt. Stir to heat through and coat evenly with sauce.

9. Add meat and vegetable mixture. Add green onions and white pepper powder. Stir and mix everything well.

In many Chinese restaurants, this dish is cooked with deep-fried noodles, which makes it crispier and tastier, but is not as healthy as the stir-fried recipe.

Stir-Fried Rice Noodles with Beef and Spinach

Ingredients

½ pound lean beef, thinly sliced

2 teaspoons cornstarch

1 teaspoon and 1 tablespoon soy sauce

1 teaspoon cooking wine

½ teaspoon salt, or to taste

10 ounces rice noodle (vermicelli), wide and thick type

3 tablespoons cooking oil

3 tablespoons oyster sauce

1 teaspoon white pepper powder or ½ teaspoon black pepper powder

10 ounces thin spinach

1 tablespoon green onion (scallions), chopped

½ teaspoon sesame oil

Directions

1. Marinate beef in 2 teaspoons of cornstarch, 1 teaspoon of soy sauce, 1 teaspoon of cooking wine, and ½ teaspoon of salt for 15 minutes.
2. Boil vermicelli in boiling water for 2–3 minutes (do not overcook). Rinse with cold water to cool, drain, and set aside.
3. Heat wok over medium-high heat and add 1 tablespoon cooking oil. When hot, add beef slices to stir-fry until color changes. Remove and set aside.
4. Add remaining oil, heat the wok until hot, add vermicelli, and stir. Add oyster sauce, soy sauce, salt, and pepper powder, stirring to heat through.
5. Add spinach to mix well with meat and noodles.
6. Add chopped green onion, tossing in sesame oil.

When cooking rice noodles, vegetables are often used to add extra flavor and nutrition to balance the meat. Mung bean sprouts, onions, cabbage, and spinach are all good choices. Mung bean is especially popular for its extra crispy texture.

Beijing-Style Noodles

Ingredients

2 tablespoons cooking oil
1 teaspoon minced garlic
2 teaspoons fresh ginger, minced
2 scallions, finely chopped
½ pound ground pork
1 tablespoon soy sauce

2 teaspoons cooking wine
3 tablespoons sweet-flour sauce/
paste or plum sauce
1 teaspoon salt, or to taste
10–12 ounces Chinese egg
noodles

Directions

1. Heat a wok over high heat. Add cooking oil and heat until hot.
2. Add garlic, ginger, and half the chopped scallions over medium heat. Stir for 30 seconds.
3. Add ground pork and stir. Add 1 tablespoon of soy sauce and cooking wine; keep stirring until meat turns to brown.
4. Add sweet-flour paste. Mix and stir with the meat until well-blended.
5. Add remaining scallions. Season with pinch of salt if necessary; continue to stir for 20 seconds.
6. Remove and place in a bowl.
7. Boil the noodles in a large saucepan according to the package directions (about 3–5 minutes or until tender but still firm). Drain and place in a large bowl.

Traditionally, the noodles and sauce are served in individual dishes, allowing each person to help themselves to noodles and then sauce to taste.

When cooking, if the sweet fermented flour paste is too thick, stir in 1 tablespoon of water.

Shredded cucumbers can be served with the noodles as a garnish. Other garnish ideas include shredded lettuce, blanched mung bean sprouts, shredded scallions, shredded spinach, and shredded radish.

Appetizers

Chinese Cabbage Dumplings
(Jiao Zi)

Ingredients

4½ cups all-purpose flour
8½ cups water
10½ ounces ground pork
4 cups finely chopped bok choy or Chinese (Napa) cabbage
1½ teaspoons salt, or to taste
2 teaspoons ginger, finely chopped

⅛ teaspoon five-spice powder or white-pepper powder
2 teaspoons oyster sauce
1 granulated chicken bouillon cube
2 tablespoons cooking oil
1 teaspoon sesame oil
3 green onions (scallions), chopped

Directions

1. Mix the flour with ½ cup of water to make dough. Knead until smooth and let stand for 30 minutes.

2. To prepare the filling, mix the meat with all the ingredients except the scallions. Stir in one direction until well-mixed. Add scallions and blend well.

3. Divide the dough into four portions and roll into long rolls. Cut each into 25 pieces. Flatten each piece and roll into 2-inch circles. Place one portion of filling in the center of each wrapper and fold the dough over it, making a bonnet-shape pouch. Pinch the edges together to seal the dumpling. Repeat until all the dough and filling are used.

4. Bring 8 cups of water in a large pot to a boil over high heat. Add half the dumplings. Stir them around gently with a ladle, and let the water return to a boil. Add enough cold water to stop the boiling, and then bring back to a boil. When the water boils again, add more cold water and bring to a boil a third time. The dumplings are done when they float to the surface. Remove, drain well, and serve.

Ready to-use jiao zi wrappers are available in most Asian supermarkets. It is much easier and more convenient to prepare jiao zi using these premade wrappers. Moisten the edges of the wrappers with water for easy, tight sealing.

Pork can be replaced with ground beef, lamb, or shrimp.

Homemade jiao zi filling always comes with some kind of vegetable for better nutrition. Bok choy, cabbage, celery, and chives are the most common ones. The name of Sanxian jiao zi ("Triple Delight") comes from mixing meat with three other raw materials, the most popular of which are mushrooms, bamboo shoots, and bok choy.

Five-spice powder is made from five spices and can be found in the seasoning section of many Asian grocery stores.

Pork and Shrimp Wontons

Ingredients

½ pound boneless lean pork
½ pound shelled and deveined medium shrimp
3 water chestnuts, peeled and finely chopped
1 teaspoon minced ginger
1 tablespoon oyster sauce

1 tablespoon light soy sauce
1 tablespoon rice cooking wine
1 teaspoon sugar
Few drops sesame oil
¼ teaspoon white pepper powder or black pepper powder
Wonton wrappers, as needed

Directions

1. Combine the pork and shrimp with the water chestnuts, ginger, oyster sauce, soy sauce, rice wine, sugar, sesame oil, and white pepper. Mix well.

2. Angle a wonton wrapper so it faces you like a diamond. (Cover the remaining wonton skins with a damp towel to keep them from drying out.) Moisten the edges of the wonton wrapper with water. Place a heaping teaspoon (about 2 teaspoons) of wonton filling in the center.

3. Form a triangle by folding the bottom tip to the top tip and pinch out as much air as possible. Press down firmly on the ends to seal. For the "boat" version, start by making the triangle wonton. Moisten either of the two side tips and fold them together, overlapping one on top of the other. The end result should be boat-like, with two tips cradling a puff of filling in the middle. Repeat with remaining wontons.

4. Boiling the wontons: Bring a large pot of water to a boil. Add the wontons, making sure there is enough room for them to move about freely. Let the wontons boil for 5–8 minutes until they rise to the top and the filling is cooked through. Remove from the pot with a slotted spoon.

This is a basic recipe for a wonton with a pork and shrimp filling.

For extra flavor and texture, use fresh water chestnuts in meat mixture.

Alternate wrapping method: Place a teaspoon of filling in the middle of the wrapper and twist to seal. The final result should resemble a money bag or drawstring purse.

Wontons can be prepared ahead of time up to the cooking stage and frozen. Thaw before cooking.

Pork and Shrimp Steamed Buns

Ingredients

Dough
1 cup warm water
3 cups all-purpose flour
2 teaspoons active dry yeast
1 tablespoon granulated sugar
1 teaspoon salt

Filling
6 ounces ground pork
1 teaspoon minced ginger
1 teaspoon salt
1 teaspoon sugar
2 teaspoons cooking wine
2 teaspoons sesame oil
2 teaspoons light soy sauce
2 teaspoons oyster sauce
1 tablespoon cooking oil
4 tablespoons water
25 medium-size shrimp, shelled, deveined, and cut into smaller pieces
1 tablespoon finely chopped green onion (scallions)

Directions

1. Mix the flour and other ingredients with water to make dough. Knead until smooth. Wrap with plastic wrap and let stand for about 2–3 hours at room temperature to allow for rising. (You can make 16–20 buns depending on the thickness of the wrap.)

2. Combine all filling ingredients (except shrimp and chopped green onion). Mix and stir in one direction until thick and sticky, then add shrimp and green onion. Mix well and put in the refrigerator for 2 hours.

3. Sprinkle work surface with flour. Put dough onto prepared surface, knead for 1 minute, and roll into a log about 16 inches long and 1½ inches wide. Divide the dough evenly into 16 portions and roll each into a ball. Using a rolling pin, roll each ball into a 3-inch-diameter-circle bun wrap (or you can flatten each ball with the palm of your hand into the shape).

4. Scoop a heaping tablespoon of filling mixture and place at the center of each dough circle. Gather up the edges to enclose the filling, then twist the edges together and seal securely. Repeat with remaining dough and filling.

5. Bring water to a rolling boil in the steamer. Place the lettuce leaves on the bottom of the steamer rack and arrange the buns on the lettuce (at least 1 inch apart and about eight for one rack).

6. Cover and steam for 15 minutes.

Lettuce leaves can be replaced by wax paper or cheesecloth.

This is a basic recipe for steamed buns. There is a huge variety in what you can make. In Chinese culture, steamed buns (baozi) are a popular food and widely available. Although it is often served as breakfast, it actually can be eaten at any meal.

An unsweetened steamed bun is usually served with a dipping sauce made from vinegar and soy sauce.

Shanghai-Style Steamed Buns

Ingredients

2 teaspoons light soy sauce
2 teaspoons oyster sauce
1 tablespoon cooking oil
4 tablespoons water
25 medium-size shrimp, shelled, deveined, and cut into smaller pieces
1 tablespoon finely chopped green onion (scallions)

Filling
6 ounces ground pork
1 teaspoon minced ginger
1 teaspoon salt
1 teaspoon sugar
2 teaspoons cooking wine
2 teaspoons sesame oil

Dough
3 cups all-purpose flour
1 cup warm water
2 teaspoons active dry yeast
1 tablespoon granulated sugar
1 teaspoon salt

Directions

1. Mix the flour and other ingredients with water to make the dough. Knead until smooth. Wrap with plastic wrap, let stand for about 2–3 hours at room temperature, and let rise (can make 16–20 buns depending on the thickness of the wrap).

2. Combine all filling ingredients (except shrimp and chopped green onion). Mix and stir in one direction until thick and sticky. Add shrimp and green onions; mix well and put in the refrigerator for 2 hours.

3. Sprinkle work surface with flour. Put dough onto prepared surface, knead 1 minute, and roll into a log about 16 inches long and 1½ inches wide. Divide the dough evenly into 16 portions and roll each into a ball. Using a rolling pin, roll it into a 3-inch-diameter-circle bun wrap (or you can flatten each ball with the palm of your hand into the shape).

4. Scoop a heaping tablespoon of filling mixture to the center of each dough circle and gather up the edges to enclose filling. Twist edges together and seal securely. Repeat with remaining dough and filling.

5. Heat a well-greased, nonstick pan until hot; arrange buns at least 1 inch apart.

6. Add ½ cup of water, bring it to a boil, and then turn heat to medium.

7. Cover the pan and cook for 10–15 minutes or until water completely evaporates and bottom of the buns turn golden brown.

Cooked in this way, the buns have a crispy crust and taste extraordinarily delicious. It's a very popular breakfast and snack food in Shanghai.

Egg Rolls

Ingredients

2 teaspoons minced ginger

1 pound ground pork

1 small onion, chopped

½ pound fresh mushrooms, sliced

½ pound bok choy (Chinese or Napa cabbage), sliced thinly, 1 inch lengthwise

½ pound fresh bean sprouts

2 green onions (scallions), chopped

2 teaspoons rice cooking wine

2 teaspoons soy sauce

½ teaspoon sugar

1 teaspoon sesame oil

2 teaspoons oyster sauce

1 tablespoon cornstarch

2 tablespoons water

1 package egg-roll wrappers (about 25 wrappers)

Oil, for frying

Salt and white pepper, to taste

Directions

1. Heat the wok. Add ginger and ground pork. Brown pork with ginger.
2. Add onion, mushrooms, bok choy, bean sprouts, and green onions to pork mixture.
3. Cook for 2–3 minutes.
4. Add rice wine, soy sauce, pepper, sugar, sesame oil, and oyster sauce.
5. Dissolve cornstarch with water. Mix well.
6. Add to pork mixture until it thickens; remove to a bowl and let cool.
7. Put a heaping tablespoon of filling mixture on each egg roll, moisten the edges with water, and roll into the shape of an egg roll (start rolling from one corner, stop in the middle, fold over the other edges, and continue rolling).
8. Add oil in a wok or frying pan and heat to medium. Put egg rolls in until they turn golden brown. Turn and cook other side until golden brown.
9. Put finished egg rolls on paper towel to drain oil.

Although pork is the most commonly used meat for egg rolls, shrimp and chicken are also very good choices, either as substitutes or mixed with pork.

Shumai

Ingredients

2 tablespoons peanut oil or cooking oil

1 garlic clove

1 teaspoon ginger, minced

1 green onion (scallion), chopped

8 ounces ground pork

¼ small cabbage, coarsely chopped

25 small shrimp, cut into smaller pieces

2 teaspoons light soy sauce

1 teaspoon oyster sauce

½ teaspoon sesame oil

1 teaspoon rice cooking wine

1 teaspoon cornstarch, dissolved in 1 teaspoon water

25 thin dumpling wrappers

10 lettuce leaves

¼ teaspoon salt

Directions

1. Place a wok over medium-high heat. Add oil, heat until hot, and then add garlic, ginger, and scallions. Stir for 5 seconds. Add ground pork and stir-fry until the meat darkens. Add onion and cabbage and stir for 2 minutes. Add shrimp, soy sauce, oyster sauce, sesame oil, rice wine, and dissolved cornstarch. Stir until mixed well (about 1 minute). Remove the wok and set aside to cool.

2. Place a dumpling wrapper on the work surface. Using your fingers, dab some water to completely moisten the surface of the wrapper.

3. Place 1 tablespoon of filling in the center. Pull up the edges of the wrapper around the filling (tucking the wrapper around the filling). Lightly tap the dumpling on the work surface to flatten the bottom.

4. Gently squeeze the center of the dumpling to make a slight indentation and force the filling to bulge a bit at the top.

5. Bring water to boil in a steamer. Place the lettuce leaves on the bottom of the steamer and arrange the dumpling on the lettuce.

6. Cover and steam for 10–12 minutes.

7. Serve hot. Serve with dumpling sauce (optional).

Shumai is a type of traditional Chinese dumpling served in dim sum. There are many varieties throughout different regions. The most well-known variety in the West is that associated with the southeastern province of Guangdong (Cantonese-style). The standard filling consists primarily of ground pork, small, whole, or chopped shrimp, shiitake mushrooms, green onion, ginger, and seasonings.

Fillings can be precooked or uncooked. An uncooked filling recipe can be found on page 54.

Shanghai-Style Shumai

Ingredients

4 dried shiitake mushrooms

¾ cup sweet rice (sticky rice)

6 ounces ground pork

20 small shrimp, coarsely chopped

⅓ cup diced bamboo shoots (optional)

1 teaspoon minced ginger

2 chopped green onions (scallions)

1 tablespoon soy sauce

1 teaspoon dark soy sauce

1 teaspoon oyster sauce

1 teaspoon sugar

1 teaspoon salt

1 teaspoon cooking wine

1 teaspoon sesame oil

2 tablespoons cooking oil

Thin wonton (dumpling) wrappers, as needed (approximately 25)

Lettuce leaves or bok choy leaves, as needed

Directions

1. Soak mushrooms in warm water for 40 minutes. Rinse and cut into small pieces.
2. Cook rice in rice cooker, setting aside to cool.
3. In a big bowl, combine all ingredients together. Mix well.
4. Place a dumpling wrapper on the work surface. Use your fingers to completely moisten the surface of the wrapper with water.
5. Place 1 tablespoon of filling in the center. Pull up the edges of the wrapper around the filling (tucking the wrapper around the filling). Lightly tap the dumpling on the work surface to flatten the bottom.
6. Gently squeeze the center of the dumpling to make a slight indentation and force the filling to bulge a bit at the top.
7. Bring water to boil in a steamer. Place the lettuce leaves on the bottom of the steamer and arrange the dumplings on the lettuce.
8. Cover and steam for 13–15 minutes.
9. Serve hot. Serve with dumpling sauce.

Chinese Chicken Wings

Ingredients

2 cups soy sauce
2 cups brown sugar
2 garlic cloves, sliced
5 pounds chicken wings, split and tips discarded

Directions

1. Stir soy sauce, brown sugar, and garlic slices together in a saucepan over medium heat. Cook and stir until the sugar melts completely. Remove from heat and allow to cool.
2. Place the chicken wings in a large bowl. Pour the soy sauce mixture over the wings and toss to coat evenly. Cover the bowl with plastic wrap. Allow chicken to marinate in the refrigerator for 8 hours or overnight.
3. Preheat an oven to 350°F.
4. Place the marinated chicken wings into a 9- by 13-inch baking dish. Cover the baking dish with aluminum foil.
5. Bake in the preheated oven until thoroughly hot (about 50 minutes). Remove the aluminum foil from the baking dish and continue baking, uncovered, for another 20 minutes. Serve hot.

Chinese-Style Stuffed Mushrooms

Ingredients

12 large fresh mushrooms
½ pound ground pork
1 tablespoon soy sauce
1 tablespoon finely chopped water chestnuts

¼ teaspoon salt
2 tablespoons chicken stock
1 teaspoon minced ginger
¼ teaspoon sugar

Directions

1. Remove stems from mushrooms. Wipe caps clean with a dry towel.
2. In a bowl, combine the pork, soy sauce, water chestnuts, salt, chicken stock, minced ginger, and sugar until thoroughly mixed.
3. Spoon stuffing tightly into mushroom caps (heaping over the cap is okay). Arrange in a steamer basket, stuffing-side up, over boiling water.
4. Cover and cook for 15 minutes. Serve hot.

These mushrooms with pork-hash stuffing are great as an appetizer or even as a side dish. The size of the mushrooms you have on hand will dictate the amount of stuffing that goes into them. Removed stems can be saved for later use.

Chinese-Style Spareribs

Ingredients

¾ tablespoon salt
7 tablespoons brown sugar
1 crushed red pepper
1 garlic clove, chopped
1 rack pork spareribs, cleaned
and excess fat removed

4 tablespoons soy sauce
3 tablespoons cooking rice wine
3 tablespoons water
1½ tablespoons Chinese dark
vinegar or any rice vinegar
1 tablespoon honey

Directions

1. Mix all dry ingredients and chopped garlic in a bowl. Rub onto ribs.
2. Put ribs in a big bowl, cover, and put in the refrigerator for 2–3 hours.
3. Mix all wet ingredients in a small bowl, put aside.
4. Preheat oven to 375°F.
5. Using heavy-duty foil, lay ribs on the sheet.
6. Pour the wet ingredients mixture onto ribs evenly. Wrap foil securely and make sure to cover ribs very well.
7. Move the wrapped ribs to a baking pan. Bake for 60 minutes.
8. Cut into single ribs. Spoon some leftover juice in the wrap to add flavor.

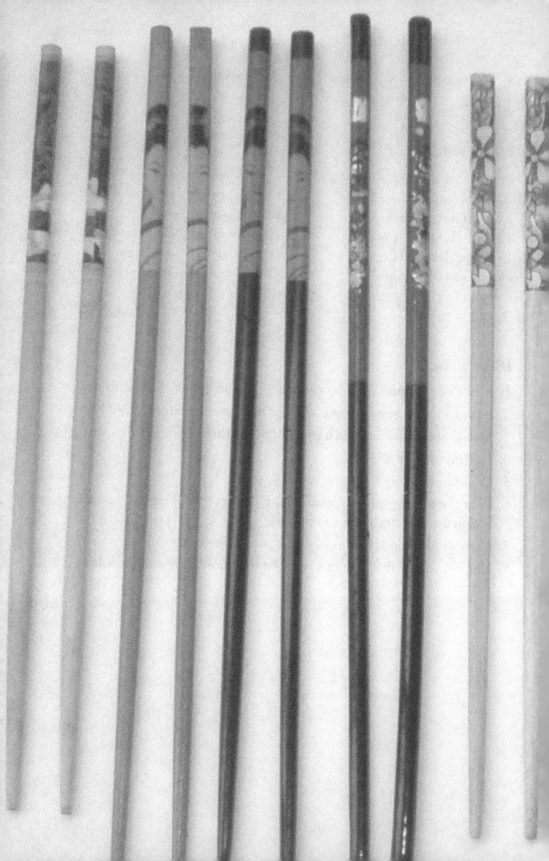

Side Dishes

Green Vegetables with Mushrooms

Ingredients

10 fresh mushrooms or 6–8 dried mushrooms

1 tablespoon cooking oil

1 clove garlic, sliced

½ pound Shanghai bok choy or tender leaves of Chinese (Napa) cabbage, washed and excess water drained

½ teaspoon salt

2 teaspoons oyster sauce

2 teaspoons cornstarch, mixed well with 2 teaspoons water

Directions

1. Soak dried mushrooms in warm water for at least 30 minutes or until soft. Clean and cut into quarters.
2. Place a wok over high heat until hot. Add 2 teaspoons of cooking oil. Add garlic slices and stir for 10 seconds.
3. Add green vegetables and stir for 2 minutes or until they shrink.
4. Add some salt and stir-fry for 20 seconds.
5. Turn off the heat. Place vegetables on a plate.
6. Clean the wok and put it over high heat again.
7. Add remaining cooking oil, and then add mushroom chunks when the oil is hot.
8. Stir-fry for about 1 minute. Add ¼ cup of water and braise on low heat until boiling. Add remaining salt, oyster sauce, and cornstarch mixture; stir and mix well.
9. Turn off the heat. Place the mushrooms over the cooked vegetables. Pour the sauce in the wok onto the green vegetables and mushrooms.

This simple and delicious dish can be used for many green vegetables, although Shanghai bok choy is the most popular one. This recipe is not only fresh in color, but it also tastes very good. It can easily be tailored to suit most palates and can be cooked year-round using simple cooking methods.

Chinese cabbage (or Napa cabbage) refers to Chinese leafy vegetables used often in Chinese cuisine. Baby bok choy, also known as Shanghai bok choy, refers to a less mature version that could develop into the white-stem variety with more time to grow before being harvested.

Stir-Fried Green Beans

Ingredients

1 tablespoon light soy sauce

½ teaspoon vinegar

½ teaspoon sesame oil

1 teaspoon sugar

2 tablespoons vegetable oil or any other cooking oil

12 ounces fresh green beans, trimmed

¾ teaspoon salt, or to taste

2 tablespoons minced ginger

1 clove garlic, sliced or minced

Directions

1. In a small bowl, mix soy sauce, vinegar, sesame oil, and sugar.
2. Heat cooking oil in a wok or sauté pan over medium-high heat until simmering.
3. Add beans. Add salt and cook, stirring constantly (about 8–10 minutes until most of the beans are shrunken and tender). Reduce heat to low and add ginger and garlic, stirring for about another minute.
4. Add soy sauce mixture to the pan. Mix well until beans are coated with the sauce.

This recipe is frequently served as a side for pork and chicken dishes. It is very easy to prepare and really delicious.

Green beans take time to turn tender. A quick method to reduce cooking time is to first boil the beans for 4–5 minutes. Drain well and then stir-fry as instructed above, but with a shorter cooking time.

Romaine Lettuce with Oyster Sauce

Ingredients

3 teaspoons cooking oil
2 cloves garlic, sliced
1 medium-size head romaine lettuce
¼ teaspoon salt
1 tablespoon oyster sauce

Directions

1. Preheat the wok over medium-high heat. Add oil. When hot, add garlic slices.
2. Turn heat to high, add lettuce, and stir quickly for about 1 minute.
3. Add salt and oyster sauce, stirring for another minute.
4. Remove to a serving plate.

This is a very simple, easy-to-make side dish. Green leafy vegetables are healthy and nutritious. Low in calories (about 10 calories per cup), they are also an excellent source of vitamin C. Broccoli is another healthy and simple variation for this dish, although it takes a little longer to cook.

Scrambled Eggs with Tomatoes

Ingredients

1 teaspoon cooking oil
3 eggs, cracked into bowl and beaten
1 green onion (scallion), chopped
2 medium-size tomatoes, cut into chunks
½ teaspoon salt
2 teaspoons light soy sauce
1 teaspoon sugar

Directions

1. Place a wok or a nonstick saucepan over high heat until hot. Add 1 teaspoon of cooking oil. Add in the beaten egg slowly when oil turns hot.

2. Stir-fry until the egg turns yellowish. Scramble it into chunks with the cooking spatula. Remove from the wok and place on a plate.

3. Place the wok over heat again and add the remaining cooking oil. When hot, add chopped onion and stir for several seconds.

4. Add tomato chunks and stir on medium-high heat for about 3–4 minutes or until you can see the juice coming out. Add in the scrambled eggs. Stir for another minute.

5. Add salt, soy sauce, and sugar. Stir evenly. Remove and serve hot.

This dish is very simple to cook and is very nutritious. It's also really eye-catching with its bright red-and-yellow color. It tastes especially fresh, with an original taste and flavor.

There are several tips for cooking this dish:

1. The proportion of egg to tomato should be preserved to make it more delicious and nutritious.

2. The eggs must be beaten well to make the color of the egg more attractive.

3. Using a little bit of sugar can neutralize the sourness of the tomatoes.

Variations of this dish all emphasize colorful appearance, appealing taste, and nutritional value. The most popular variations are Scrambled Eggs with Cucumber on page 67 (yellow-green in color) and Scrambled Eggs with Black Wood-Ear Mushrooms on page 66.

Scrambled Eggs with Black Wood-Ear Mushrooms

Ingredients

1 handful dried black wood-ear mushrooms

1 tablespoon cooking oil

2 eggs, well-beaten

1 tablespoon chopped green onion (scallions)

1 carrot, peeled and cut into thin slices or diamond-shape slices

½ teaspoon salt, or to taste

½ teaspoon white-pepper powder or black-pepper powder

½ teaspoon sesame oil

Directions

1. Soak black wood-ear mushrooms in warm water for 45–60 minutes to fully expand and soften. Clean, trim off the roots, and tear into smaller pieces.

2. Heat 1 teaspoon of cooking oil in a nonstick wok. Add the beaten eggs. Cook on medium heat until the eggs completely set. Use spatula to scramble eggs into smaller pieces. Remove from the wok, setting aside.

3. Heat remaining oil in wok. Add green onions and stir for 10 seconds

4. Add the carrot slices and black wood-ear mushrooms. Stir over high heat for 2 minutes.

5. Add salt, cooking for one minute. Turn heat to medium, add the eggs, and stir for another minute.

6. Turn off the heat. Add white pepper powder and sesame oil.

7. Place everything on a serving plate. Serve hot.

This dish is delicious and can be served either as an entrée or side dish. Besides the appealing colors, the fluffiness of the eggs provides a textural contrast to the crispy black wood-ear mushrooms.

Scrambled Eggs with Cucumber

Ingredients

1 tablespoon cooking oil
2 eggs, beaten
1 tablespoon green onion
(scallions), chopped
1 small carrot, cut into thin slices
(optional)

1 English cucumber, cleaned and
cut into thin slices
½ teaspoon salt, or to taste
¼ teaspoon white pepper powder
or black pepper powder
2 teaspoons light soy sauce
2 teaspoons oyster sauce
Several drops sesame oil

Directions

1. Place a wok over medium heat. Add 1 teaspoon of cooking oil and heat until hot. Turn heat to medium and add beaten egg. Cook until egg completely sets and use a spatula to cut eggs into chunks. Remove from the wok and set aside.

2. Add remaining oil to wok and heat until hot. Add green onion. Add carrot and cucumber slices, and stir-fry for 2 minutes.

3. Add salt, pepper powder, soy sauce, and oyster sauce, stirring for another minute.

4. Add scrambled eggs, mixing well with other ingredients.

5. Add sesame oil and stir-fry for another 45 seconds.

6. Remove and place on a serving plate. Serve hot.

This dish is characterized by its color and unique texture. It is a very typical homemade dish that can serve as either a side dish or an entrée. The crispy cucumber and tender eggs not only complement each other in taste, but they are also nutritious.

Szechuan-Style Eggplant in Garlic Sauce

Ingredients

1 tablespoon dark soy sauce

1 tablespoon sugar

1 tablespoon vinegar

1 teaspoon salt

1 tablespoon cornstarch, mixed with 3 tablespoons water

2 medium-size Chinese eggplants, cut into ½- by 2-inch strips and soaked in water

3 tablespoons oil

1 tablespoon Szechuan chili pepper paste or Szechuan chili–broad bean paste

2 cloves garlic, minced

2 teaspoons minced ginger

1 tablespoon green onion (scallions), chopped

½ teaspoon sesame oil

Directions

1. In a small bowl, mix soy sauce, sugar, vinegar, salt, and cornstarch, and set aside.

2. Drain eggplant and pat dry with paper towels.

3. Preheat wok over high heat until hot. Add 2 tablespoons of cooking oil; when hot, add eggplant. Stir-fry until seared and tender (about 5–6 minutes).

4. Add remaining cooking oil to wok, reheating wok over medium heat. Add chili paste; stir until fragrant, and add garlic, ginger, and half the green onion.

5. Add sauce mixture and stir for 20 seconds (or until thickened).

6. Turn heat to high and add eggplant. Stir quickly until most of the sauce is absorbed into the eggplant (about 1–2 minutes). Toss in sesame oil and remaining green onion.

7. Remove to serving dish. Serve hot.

Chinese eggplant varieties are commonly shaped like a narrower, slightly pendulous cucumber. If you can't find this variety, feel free to use whichever eggplant is available.

This dish is spicy, soft, and juicy. Spicy garlic sauce is one of the most popular home-style flavors and can be used in many dishes.

Szechuan chili pepper paste/sauce or Szechuan chili–broad bean paste/sauce can both be found in many Asian groceries.

Braised Baby Cabbage in Broth

Ingredients

2 teaspoons peanut oil
1 clove garlic, thinly sliced
1 cup chicken broth
10 ounces baby cabbage, cut into quarters
1 Chinese green pepper or any small-size green pepper, seeds discarded and cut into small cubes

2 teaspoons cornstarch, mixed with a little water
1 tablespoon chopped green onion (scallions)
Pinch white pepper powder
Salt, to taste

Directions

1. Heat the wok over high heat. Add oil and heat until hot.
2. Add garlic slices and stir for 5 seconds.
3. Pour in the chicken broth and bring to a boil.
4. Add baby cabbage and boil for 3–4 minutes or until the cabbage turns soft.
5. Remove cabbage quarters; place into a serving bowl.
6. Add the green pepper cubes, boiling for 1 minute.
7. Add salt and cornstarch to thicken the broth. Turn off the heat and pour the broth over the cabbage.
8. Sprinkle in chopped green onion and white pepper powder.

This simple yet healthy dish tastes fresh and silky. The authentic recipe for this dish uses a preserved egg (found in many Asian groceries), which is cut into little cubes and added into the broth with the baby cabbage. It is believed to nourish the stomach and relieve internal heat. It is a popular dish in summer.

Winter Melon with Ham and Dried Shrimp

Ingredients

2 teaspoons peanut oil
1 tablespoon chopped green onion (scallions)
2 slices ginger
6–8 ounces fresh winter melon,
peeled and cut into 2-inch cubes
15 medium-size dry shrimp,
soaked in warm water for 5–10
minutes

1 teaspoon salt, or to taste
½ cup chicken stock
½ teaspoon white-pepper powder
or black-pepper powder
3 slices ham, cut into shreds

Directions

1. Place a wok over medium-high heat until hot.
2. Add cooking oil, half the chopped green onion, and ginger. Fry for 10 seconds until fragrant.
3. Add winter melon and soaked shrimp. Stir for 1 minute.
4. Add salt, chicken stock, and pepper powder.
5. Add ham shreds.
6. Cook until water evaporates and winter melons turn tender.
7. Sprinkle in the remaining chopped green onions.
8. Remove and place in a serving bowl.

This is a popular simple yet delicious home-cooked dish, which is characterized by its fresh, smooth texture. The three main ingredients complement each other perfectly. Whereas the dried shrimp and ham enhance the flavor of winter melon, the melon, on the other hand, gives a color contrast to the ham and makes the dried shrimp milder and tastier.

Sautéed Potato, Green Pepper, and Eggplant

Ingredients

1 teaspoon cooking oil, for dish

1 cup cooking oil, for frying potatoes, eggplant, and pepper

3 medium-size potatoes, peeled and diced

1 eggplant, diced

1 green pepper, deseeded and diced

1 teaspoon ginger, chopped

1 clove garlic, sliced

1 tablespoon chopped green onion (scallions)

1 teaspoon salt, or to taste

1 teaspoon sugar

2 teaspoons soy sauce

2 teaspoons cornstarch, mixed with 1 tablespoon water

Directions

1. Heat wok over high heat.

2. Add cooking oil and heat wok until hot, turning heat to medium high.

3. Add potato pieces; stir well and fry until potatoes turn a golden brown. Remove from the wok and set aside.

4. Repeat step to fry eggplant.

5. Quick-fry the green pepper (20 seconds should be sufficient).

6. Leave 1 teaspoon of cooking oil in the wok. Add ginger, garlic, and green onion, and stir for 10 seconds.

7. Add potatoes, eggplant, and green pepper. Stir-fry for 2–3 minutes.

8. Add salt, sugar, soy sauce, and cornstarch mixture. Stir to thicken.

9. Remove from the wok and place on a serving plate. Serve hot.

Crispy Cucumber with Smashed Garlic

Ingredients

4 small cucumbers
½ teaspoon salt, or to taste
1 teaspoon light soy sauce
1 teaspoon sugar
2 teaspoons white rice vinegar or any rice vinegar

1½ teaspoons chili oil (optional)
Several drops Szechuan peppercorn oil (optional)
½ teaspoon sesame oil
2 cloves garlic, mashed

Directions

1. Peel cucumber (optional). Remove seeds and cut into large chunks.
2. Salt cucumber and put into the refrigerator for 20 minutes. Drain excess water.
3. Combine salt, soy sauce, sugar, vinegar, chili oil, Szechuan peppercorn oil, sesame oil, and mashed garlic in a large bowl. Stir and mix well.
4. Combine cucumber and sauce. Mix well.

This is a simple dish, which is easy to prepare and holds up well. The sweet crispness of the cucumber balances the bite of the garlic and the heat of the chili oil.

Celery and Dried-Tofu Shreds with Peanuts

Ingredients

½ cup peanuts
1 cup water
½ teaspoon salt, or to taste
3 stalks fresh celery, cleaned and cut into shreds
½ pack dried tofu, cut into thin shreds
1 green onion (scallion), chopped

1 teaspoon ginger, minced
3 teaspoons vegetable oil or other cooking oil
6–8 red chilies, shredded
½ teaspoon rice vinegar (white rice vinegar preferred), or to taste
Several drops Szechuan peppercorn oil (optional)

Directions

1. Put peanuts in a bowl. Add 1 cup of water and ¼ teaspoon of salt. Place the bowl into a microwave oven; microwave for 4–5 minutes or until fully cooked. Rinse with cold water to cool and drain excess water.

2. Fill a saucepan or wok half-full of water, bringing it to a boil. Pour in celery shreds. Stir and boil for 1 minute. Remove from the pan, rinse with cold water, and then drain the water by using a colander. Place on a serving plate.

3. Repeat the same steps to process the dried-tofu shreds.

4. Mix celery, tofu shreds, and peanuts in the plate. Place chopped green onion, ginger, and salt on top.

5. Heat wok with 3 teaspoons of oil, heating until hot. Add chili shreds. Turn off the heat.

6. Pour hot oil directly onto the plate.

7. Add vinegar and Szechuan peppercorn oil. Mix well.

This recipe tastes fresh and crispy, with appealing green, white, and red colors.

Celery and tofu are widely used in Chinese cooking. They can be either stir-fried, (with or without meat) or just made into a fine cold dish after being boiled briefly. The cold dish is simple to cook and has a unique, fresh flavor.

Dried tofu is available at most Asian supermarkets; either five-spice-flavor varieties or plain white curd can be used in this dish.

Szechuan peppercorn has a unique aroma and flavor that is not hot or pungent like black, white, or chili peppers. Instead, it has slight lemony overtones and creates a tingly numbness in the mouth. Both peppercorn and peppercorn oil are essential ingredients for Szechuan cuisine. It can be found in many Asian grocery stores.

Spinach with Roasted Sesame Seeds

Ingredients

1 bag spinach (about 6–8 ounces)
1 tablespoon white roasted sesame seeds
3 teaspoons cooking oil
6–8 red chili shreds
Salt, to taste

Directions

1. Rinse spinach and cut leaves lengthwise into halves.
2. Half-fill a saucepan or wok with water, bringing to a boil. Add the spinach, stir, and blanch for 30 seconds.
3. Remove from pan. Rinse with cold water to cool.
4. Drain excess water; place on a serving plate.
5. Spread salt and sesame seeds over spinach.
6. Heat wok until hot, add cooking oil and heating it until hot. Add chili shreds. Turn off heat when chili color begins to darken.
7. Pour hot oil and chili over spinach.
8. Stir and mix well, serving cold.

This sesame-spinach cold dish is fresh and tasty with an attractive green color. It is a good appetizer in the heat of summer. Spinach is rich in beta-carotene, iron, and vitamin B6. It can either be stir-fried or made into a fine cold dish after a brief blanching.

Assorted Vegetable Dish

Ingredients

½ package dried tofu, shredded
1 Asian or English cucumber, peeled and cut into shreds
½ radish, shredded
1 green chili, deseeded and shredded
1 teaspoon minced ginger

1 clove garlic, finely chopped
2 teaspoons vegetable oil
1 teaspoon rice vinegar
2 teaspoons light soy sauce
½ teaspoon sesame oil
1 teaspoon sugar
½ teaspoon salt, or to taste

Directions

1. Half-fill a saucepan with water, bringing it to a boil. Add shredded tofu to water, stir, and cook for 1 minute. Remove and drain water. Cool for awhile.
2. Mix all vegetables and tofu shreds in a bowl.
3. Mix all seasonings in a small bowl.
4. Heat the wok. Add cooking oil and heat until hot. Pour into the seasoning bowl, mix, and pour over the vegetables.
5. Stir and mix everything well. Serve cold.

This Chinese assorted-vegetable cold dish is healthy and easy to make. All of the ingredients are fresh and nutritious; this is a very refreshing dish in the summer. For extra flavor, you can always sprinkle in some roasted sesame seeds.

Bean-Sprout Cold Dish

Ingredients

1 medium carrot, peeled and cut
into thin shreds
1 stalk celery, cut into thin shreds
½ pound bean sprouts
½ teaspoon roasted sesame seeds

Dressing
½ teaspoon salt, or to taste
1 teaspoon sugar
2 teaspoons vinegar
1 teaspoon sesame oil
1 teaspoon chili oil (optional)
Dash freshly ground
white pepper

Directions

1. Bring a pot of water to a boil. Blanch all vegetables. Remove from the pot and rinse with cold water. Drain well.
2. Combine the dressing ingredients in a small bowl. Mix well and set aside.
3. Combine the vegetables with the dressing. Mix well.
4. Place in a serving bowl. Sprinkle with sesame seeds and serve cold.

You should blanch each vegetable separately until they are crisply tender; you do not want to overcook them.

You can find bean sprouts in Asian supermarkets. Be sure to pick sprouts that look clean, fresh, and crisp. Using cold water to rinse blanched bean sprouts will help to keep them fresh.

Asparagus Salad

Ingredients

1 pound asparagus, cut in half or diagonally
2 tablespoons light soy sauce
1 teaspoon sesame oil
1 teaspoon oyster sauce
1 clove garlic, fine chopped
¼ teaspoon salt, or to taste

Directions

1. Half fill a saucepan with water; bring it to a boil.
2. Add asparagus. Boil for 1–2 minutes (do not overcook). Drain and cool. Set aside.
3. Mix all other ingredients in a small bowl. Pour over the asparagus.

This is a very simple, nutritious dish—zero cholesterol and an excellent source of folic acid and potassium.

The dressing can be prepared in advance and kept in a covered jar in the refrigerator (do not freeze).

Lotus Root in Sweet and Sour Sauce

Ingredients

12 ounces lotus root (about 2 medium-size pieces), peeled and cut into thin slices

1 medium carrot, peeled and cut into thin slices

2 teaspoons chopped green onion (scallions)

1 teaspoon minced ginger

½ teaspoon salt

2 tablespoons sugar

2 tablespoons vinegar (white rice vinegar preferred)

2 teaspoons cooking oil

Directions

1. In a saucepan, add enough water to cover lotus-root pieces and bring water to a boil. Add lotus root slices; cook for 1 minute.
2. Add carrot slices to water, cooking for another minute.
3. Remove and soak in cold water to cool. Drain well and put on a serving plate.
4. Put chopped green onion and ginger on top.
5. Mix salt, sugar, and vinegar. Pour onto the plate.
6. Place a wok over high heat until hot. Add cooking oil. Pour oil onto the lotus root and carrot.
7. Stir well. Serve cold.

The lotus root is a root vegetable that is indigenous to Asia and is found underwater. Similar in shape to a long squash, it is common for lotus roots to grow very long. Preparation of this food involves removing the skin to reveal the white interior. The meat has a texture that is slightly crunchy and mildly sweet. Lotus root can be found in most Asian supermarkets during the summer season. This recipe has a crisp, refreshing taste, and looks appealing with red and white coloration.

It is a good dish on hot summer days, since lotus root is believed to help with relieving heat and sunstroke. In addition to being eaten cold, lotus root can also be cooked to make a variety of warm dishes.

Steamed Eggplant with Garlic and Sesame Paste

Ingredients

3 Chinese eggplants or any eggplants, halved lengthwise and cut into thick strips

2 teaspoons sesame paste

½ teaspoon salt, or to taste

2 teaspoons garlic, finely minced

1 teaspoon minced ginger

1 teaspoon vinegar

½ teaspoon sesame oil

2 teaspoons water

1 teaspoon sugar

Directions

1. Place eggplant on a plate and put into a boiling steamer. Steam for 10 minutes or until tender.
2. Remove from the steamer. Cool.
3. Mix sesame paste, salt, garlic, ginger, vinegar, sesame oil, water, and sugar in a small bowl.
4. Pour onto eggplant and stir. Serve cold.

Eggplant is a great addition to one's diet, because they are high in fiber, vitamin K, and vitamin B6 while being low in saturated fat. This eggplant dish is simple and quick to make. It can be either served with rice as a main dish for a vegetarian meal or as a side dish with meat. If you are a fan of eggplant, you're sure to enjoy this recipe.

Chicken with Vegetables

Ingredients

2 chicken breasts
1 medium onion, thinly shredded
1 stalk celery, thinly shredded
1 medium carrot, peeled and
thinly shredded
2 teaspoons cooking oil
1 clove garlic, chopped
1 teaspoon ginger, minced

Seasoning
1 teaspoon salt
2 teaspoons light soy sauce
1 teaspoon white vinegar
2 teaspoons sugar
½ teaspoon freshly ground white
pepper
1 teaspoon sesame oil
½ teaspoon Szechuan peppercorn oil (optional)
1½ teaspoons chili oil (optional,
or to taste)

Directions

1. Rinse the chicken breast, removing any excess fat.
2. Bring a pot of water to a boil. Put chicken breasts into the pot and boil for 8–10 minutes. Remove from the pot and let cool. Shred into pieces.
3. Combine all seasoning ingredients in a bowl. Mix well.
4. Combine all vegetables and chicken breast shreds in a serving bowl.
5. Combine the vegetable/chicken shreds with the seasonings. Mix well.
6. Add cooking oil to a wok and heat until hot. Add chopped garlic and ginger, and stir for 20 seconds. Pour hot oil directly onto chicken/vegetables. Serve cold.

This is an easy-to-prepare, refreshing, and healthy cold dish, and balances well with white meat and vegetables.

Szechuan-Style Chicken Salad

Ingredients

1 pound chicken breast (organic preferred), excess fat removed and rinsed clean

2 tablespoons sesame seed paste

2 tablespoons soy sauce

1 tablespoon vinegar

½ tablespoon sesame oil

½ teaspoon roasted Szechuan peppercorn or ½ teaspoon Szechuan peppercorn oil (optional)

1 tablespoon hot chili oil (optional)

3 teaspoons sugar

1 small Asian cucumber, cut into slices and lightly salted

1 medium carrot, cut into thin shreds

1 tablespoon green onion (scallions), finely chopped

Directions

1. In a saucepan, add enough water to cover chicken. Bring to a boil; add chicken. Bring water to a boil again and cook for 12 minutes. Remove and cool.

2. Cut chicken into small strips as thick as chopsticks.

3. In a small bowl, mix together sesame seed paste, soy sauce, rice vinegar, sesame oil, Szechuan peppercorn oil, chili oil, and sugar.

4. Arrange the cucumber slices on a serving plate. Add chicken on top and pour the sauce over. Garnish with carrot shreds and green onion.

Any precooked (roasted, smoked, or poached) chicken is a good option for this dish.

Sesame seed paste can be replaced with peanut butter (or even almond butter).

To add even more flavor to this dish, feel free to garnish with roasted sesame seeds or chopped roasted peanuts before serving. This will enhance the taste as well as give it an authentic Szechuan appeal.

Black Wood-Ear Mushrooms with Celery

Ingredients

1 handful dried black wood-ear mushrooms
3 stems celery, halved and then cut into 1-inch-long sections
½ red bell pepper, shredded
1 teaspoon sesame oil

1 teaspoon salt
1 teaspoon vinegar
2 teaspoons cooking oil
1 teaspoon minced ginger
1 clove garlic, chopped

Directions

1. Soak black wood-ear mushrooms in warm water for 30–50 minutes or until they soften. Rinse, trimming the ends. Add water in a saucepan and bring to a boil. Add black wood-ear mushrooms and boil for 3 minutes. Rinse with cold water and drain. Set aside.

2. Boil water in the saucepan again, add celery, and cook for 1 minute. Rinse with cold water. Drain well.

3. Combine red pepper, celery, and black wood-ear mushrooms in a salad dish. Add sesame oil, salt, and vinegar.

4. Heat wok until hot. Add cooking oil. Add ginger and garlic.

5. Pour oil directly onto vegetables, mixing well. Serve cold.

Celery is considered a great remedy for high blood pressure. This dish can help in lowering blood pressure, removing fat, and losing weight.

Soups

Chicken Tofu and Vegetable Soup

Ingredients

½ pound boneless, skinless chicken breast

3½ cups chicken stock

4 egg whites

2 teaspoons soybean powder or 1 teaspoon cornstarch

12 spinach leaves or 16 snow pea tips

⅓ teaspoon white pepper powder or ¼ teaspoon black pepper powder

2 tablespoons diced ham

Salt, to taste

Directions

1. Clean chicken breast and cut into small pieces, then chop into a ground mixture. Put in a bowl; pour in ½ cup of cold chicken stock to loosen the meat.

2. Beat egg white until frothy. Add ¼ teaspoon of salt and soybean powder. Stir well.

3. Combine egg-white mixture and chicken mixture. Stir and mix well.

4. Add chicken stock in a saucepan, bringing to a boil.

5. Turn heat to low and pour in the chicken mixture. Gently stir several times to make sure the chicken has been completely covered by the soup. Simmer until chicken becomes jelly-like pieces (about 2–3 minutes).

6. Add spinach leaves (or snow pea tips) on the top, covering the pan for 1 minute. Sprinkle a little bit of white pepper powder on top.

7. Spread ham on the bottom of the serving bowl. Pour soup in the bowl. Serve hot.

This Chinese chicken soup is made with boneless, skinless chicken breast. It is simple to make, though you should still be careful. The chicken is delicate, tender, and as soft as silken tofu (literally chicken tofu). The soup is fresh and delicious with bright-green color.

Contrary to their name, snow pea tips do not actually refer to the tips of the pods. Rather, the name refers to the leafy growth near the pods. If you are buying prebagged snow pea tips from a Chinese grocer, look for bags that do not contain too many curly tendrils, which you will need to pick away.

Chinese Chicken Corn Soup

Ingredients

4 ounces boneless, skinless
chicken breast
1 teaspoon Chinese cooking wine
¼ teaspoon salt
1 teaspoon cornstarch
3 cups chicken stock

½ cup water
1 teaspoon light soy sauce
½ onion, cut into small pieces
1 cup sweet corn
Salt, to taste

Directions

1. Clean and cut chicken into small pieces. Mix with 1 teaspoon of cooking wine, ¼ teaspoon of salt, and 1 teaspoon of cornstarch.

2. Add chicken stock, water, soy sauce, onion, and sweet corn in a saucepan. Bring to a boil.

3. Add chicken-breast pieces, stirring to separate. Cover and simmer for 10 minutes over low heat.

4. Add salt to taste. Turn off heat and serve hot.

If chicken stock is not available, you can use 3 cups of water and mix with two chicken bouillon cubes.

Chinese cooking wine is made from rice, so it is also known as rice cooking wine. It can be found in the seasoning section of most Asian grocery stores or supermarkets. You probably will see both white and dark varieties, although they are typically interchangeable, with the dark one having a stronger flavor.

Chinese Egg-Drop Soup

Ingredients

4 cups chicken broth or stock

2 eggs, lightly beaten

Few drops sesame oil

¼ teaspoon Chinese white pepper powder or black pepper powder

1 green onion (scallion), finely chopped

Salt, to taste

Directions

1. In a soup pot or saucepan, add chicken broth or stock. Bring to a boil.
2. Slowly pour in the eggs in a steady stream. Gently stir the eggs in a clockwise direction to make thin streams.
3. Sprinkle sesame oil and white pepper powder. Garnish with chopped green onion on top. Serve hot.

Chinese egg-drop soup is a very popular soup in Chinese restaurants and is frequently thickened with cornstarch. To add a cornstarch thickener, mix 2–3 tablespoons of cornstarch with ½ cup of water. Just before adding the beaten egg, stir in the cornstarch-water mixture, remove the soup from the heat, and then add the beaten egg.

The basic recipe for egg-drop soup is very simple, and there are many popular variations. Homemade egg-drop soup usually adds vegetables such as tomatoes, cucumbers, and seaweed to make it healthier and tastier.

Tomato Egg-Drop Soup

Ingredients

½ tablespoon cooking oil

2 medium-size tomatoes, cleaned and diced

1 teaspoon light soy sauce

1 teaspoon salt, or to taste

2 cups water

2 cups chicken stock

2 tablespoons cornstarch, mixed well with ½ cup water

1 large egg, beaten well

2 teaspoons chopped green onion (scallions)

Several drops sesame oil

Directions

1. Heat oil in the wok over high heat; add tomato pieces, soy sauce, and salt. Stir-fry for 1 minute; turn heat to medium-high, cover, and simmer until tomato becomes very soft and juice comes out.

2. Add water (boiling water preferred) and chicken stock. Bring to a boil, and then add mixed cornstarch and stir quickly to thicken the soup.

3. Slowly pour in the egg in a steady stream while gently stirring in a clockwise direction. The egg will begin to feather and spread.

4. Garnish with chopped green onion and sprinkle sesame oil on top. Remove from the heat and serve hot.

If you don't like thick soup, add less cornstarch and more water/stock.

Cucumber Egg-Drop Soup

Ingredients

½ tablespoon cooking oil
1 teaspoon minced fresh ginger
1 green onion (scallion), finely chopped
2 cups soup stock
2 cups water
½ English cucumber, cleaned and cut into thin slices

2 tablespoons cornstarch, mixed with 4 tablespoons water
½ teaspoon salt, or to taste
1 large egg, beaten well
½ teaspoon white pepper powder or ⅓ teaspoon black pepper powder
Several drops sesame oil

Directions

1. Heat oil in the saucepan; add ginger and half the green onion.
2. Add stock and water, bringing to a boil.
3. Add cucumber, pour in cornstarch mixture, and stir well to thicken the soup.
4. Add salt; bring to a boil. Slowly pour in the egg in a steady stream while gently stirring in a clockwise direction. The egg will begin to feather and spread.
5. Sprinkle white pepper powder and sesame oil. Garnish with remaining chopped green onion. Serve hot.

Seaweed Egg-Drop Soup with Tofu

Ingredients

2 cups soup stock

2 cups water

½ box Chinese soft tofu (silken tofu), cut into small cubes

½ teaspoon salt, or to taste

½ teaspoon white pepper powder or ⅓ teaspoon black pepper powder

2 tablespoons cornstarch, mixed with 4 tablespoons water

¼ English cucumber (or 1 Asian cucumber), cut into thin slices

1 ounce dried Chinese seaweed, torn into smaller pieces

1 egg, beaten well

1 tablespoon chopped green onion (scallions)

Drops sesame oil

Directions

1. Add soup stock and water in a saucepan, bringing to a boil.
2. Add tofu, cooking for 2 minutes.
3. Add salt and pepper.
4. Add cornstarch to thicken the soup.
5. Add cucumber slices and seaweed.
6. Bring the soup back to a boil, and then lower the heat.
7. Pour in the egg. Stir quickly in a clockwise direction. The egg will begin to feather and spread.
8. Turn off the heat. Garnish with chopped onion and sprinkle sesame oil on top.

A great combination and easy to make, this homemade recipe is both healthy and nutritious.

Seaweed includes several groups of multicellular algae—red algae, green algae, and brown algae—which can be eaten and used in the preparation of food. Seaweed typically contains high amounts of fiber and protein, and is used extensively in soup or to wrap sushi in China, Japan, and Korea. You can find seaweed in many Asian grocery stores. Most commonly used seaweeds are sheets of the dried red algae Porphyra.

Tomato and Silken Tofu Soup

Ingredients

2 teaspoons cooking oil
1 teaspoon fresh minced ginger
2 large tomatoes, peeled and cut
into small pieces
3½ cups soup stock
½ box silken tofu, cut into small
cubes

1 teaspoon salt, or to taste
¼ teaspoon white pepper powder
or black pepper powder
2 teaspoons finely chopped green
onion (scallions)

Directions

1. Heat oil in a saucepan. Add minced ginger. Stir for 20 seconds, and then add tomatoes.
2. Cook for 3 minutes, and then add enough soup stock to cover the tomatoes. Bring to a boil on high heat. Lower the heat to a simmer and cook for 5–7 minutes.
3. Add remaining soup stock. Bring to a boil, add tofu pieces, and cook for about 2 minutes.
4. Add salt to taste. Sprinkle pepper and chopped green onion on top. Serve hot.

Tofu and tomatoes are two very healthy soup ingredients. Tomatoes are considered one of the top-10 cancer-fighting foods. Nutritious and packed with antioxidants, they are also believed to help in lowering blood pressure and cholesterol.

Blanching tomatoes with hot water will help to remove the skins. However, removing the skins is optional.

Hot and Sour Soup

Ingredients

2 ounces shredded pork tender-loin

1 teaspoon soy sauce

½ teaspoon sesame oil

1 teaspoon cornstarch

6 dried black wood-ear mush-rooms

1 tablespoon cooking oil

1 teaspoon minced fresh ginger

2 cups water

2 cups soup stock

½ cup bamboo shoots, cut into thin strips

3–4 dried or fresh shiitake mush-rooms

¼ box soft tofu, cut into small cubes

1½ teaspoons salt, or to taste

1 teaspoon granulated sugar

2 tablespoons soy sauce

2½ tablespoons rice vinegar

2 tablespoons cornstarch, mixed well with ¼ cup water

1 egg, beaten

1 green onion (scallion), finely chopped

White pepper, to taste (no more than 1 tablespoon)

⅓ teaspoon sesame oil

Chili oil, to taste

Pinch salt

Directions

1. Marinate pork in 1 teaspoon of soy sauce, ½ teaspoon of sesame oil, 1 teaspoon of cornstarch, and a pinch of salt.

2. Soak mushrooms in warm water for 35 minutes or until softened. Rinse, remove unwanted stems, and cut into thin shreds.

3. Heat 1 tablespoon of cooking oil in a wok. Add minced ginger.

4. Add shredded pork, stir-fry until cooked. Remove and place on a plate, setting aside.

5. Boil water and soup stock in a saucepan; add bamboo shoots, black wood-ear mushrooms, and shiitake mushrooms. Bring to a boil again.

6. Add tofu and precooked pork shreds; stir in salt, sugar, soy sauce, and vinegar. Taste the broth and adjust the taste if desired.

7. Slowly pour the cornstarch mixture into the soup, stirring while it is being added until the soup thickens.

8. Return the broth to a boil, and then turn down the heat. Slowly drop in the beaten egg, stirring in one direction at the same time. Add chopped green onion and white pepper.

9. Add chili oil. Drizzle with sesame oil. Serve hot.

Hot and sour soup is reputed to be good for colds. For a vegetarian version, leave out the pork. Pork can also be replaced by shredded ham, and in this case, there is no need to precook.

Black wood-ear mushrooms, also known as black fungus or tree ears, are an edible fungus used primarily in Asian cuisine. Like tofu, black wood-ear mushrooms have no flavor of their own, but soak in the flavors that they are cooked with. The delicate, crinkly mushrooms are also valued for their crunchy texture. You'll often find them added to hot and sour soup, and are also featured in many stir-fried dishes. Popular in China, where use of food for medicinal purposes is common, a soup or dish containing this mushroom species is used for the treatment of diabetes and high cholesterol. Black wood-ear mushrooms are sold mainly in dried form in many Asian grocery stores.

Before using, soak the mushrooms in warm water for at least 15 minutes. They will puff up to several times their normal size. Rinse and trim the stems before cutting.

Chicken with Mushroom Soup

Ingredients

20 pieces dried straw mushrooms
2 cups water
6 thin slices ginger
1 green onion (scallion), cut into sections
1 teaspoon Chinese rice vinegar

¼ organic chicken with bone and skin, cleaned and excess fat removed, then cut into chunks
3 cups soup stock
2 teaspoons rice wine
½ onion, cut into small pieces
2 carrots, cut into cubes
1 teaspoon salt, or to taste

Directions

1. Soak mushrooms in warm water for 40 minutes or until softened. Rinse well and cut in half.
2. Boil water in a saucepan, enough to cover the chicken. Add 3 slices of ginger, green-onion sections, vinegar, and chicken chunks, and bring back to a boil. Remove chicken and drain with colander.
3. Add soup stock and water in a soup pot, bringing to a boil. Add chicken, mushrooms, rice wine, and ginger.
4. Bring to a boil, then turn heat down to simmer for 50 minutes.
5. Add onion and carrot. Continue cooking for 20 minutes.
6. Add salt to taste, cover, and let sit for 15 minutes. Serve hot.

Straw mushrooms, also called paddy straw mushrooms, have a unique flavor that distinguishes them from other mushrooms. Canned straw mushroom can be easily found in many Asian grocery stores and can be ordered online. In this recipe, only dried ones are used.

If you have an electric rice cooker, this soup is very easy to prepare. Set the cooking time to 1 hour. You can even do it before you go to work in the morning! That way, the mushroom-chicken soup is ready when you come back from work.

Chicken with Enoki Mushroom Soup

Ingredients

1 boneless, skinless chicken breast (organic preferred)

2 teaspoons cooking wine

1¼ teaspoons salt, or to taste

3 cups soup stock

1 cup hot water

3 slices thinly cut fresh ginger

1 pack fresh enoki mushrooms or oyster mushrooms (about 6 ounces), roots removed and rinsed clean

¼ teaspoon white pepper powder or black pepper powder

1 green onion (scallion), finely chopped

Directions

1. Clean chicken and cut into small cubes. Marinate with 2 teaspoons of cooking wine and ¼ teaspoon of salt.

2. In a soup pot or saucepan, add soup stock and hot water. Bring to a boil, and add ginger slices and chicken pieces.

3. Bring soup back to a boil. Then turn heat to low, cover and let simmer for 30 minutes.

4. Add enoki mushrooms, salt, and white pepper. Bring to a boil again and cook another 10–15 minutes.

5. Sprinkle chopped green onion on top and serve hot.

Enoki, which means "golden needle mushroom" in Chinese, are long, thin white mushrooms used in east Asian cuisine. It is available fresh or canned. Always use fresh enoki with firm, white, shiny caps, and avoid those that have slimy or brownish stalks. Enoki mushrooms have a crisp texture, and possess antioxidants and large quantities of protein.

Winter Melon and Meatball Soup

Ingredients

Meatballs
½ pound ground pork
1 tablespoon cornstarch
1 egg
1 teaspoon fresh minced ginger
½ teaspoon sesame oil
½ teaspoon salt
2 teaspoons oyster sauce
2 tablespoons soup stock

Soup
1 tablespoon cooking oil
1 clove garlic, sliced
4 slices fresh ginger
1 pound winter melon, peeled
and deseeded, then cut into
2-inch long by 1½-inch wide by
½-inch thick slices
1 teaspoon salt, or to taste
3 cups hot water or soup stock
1 teaspoon white pepper powder or ½ teaspoon black pepper
powder
¼ teaspoon sesame oil
1 tablespoon finely chopped
green onion (scallions)
2 stems cilantro, chopped (optional)

Directions

Meatballs

Combine all ingredients together; mix and stir the mixture in one direction until mixture becomes very sticky. Set aside.

Soup

1. Heat a saucepan, adding cooking oil, garlic, and ginger. Stir for 15 seconds.
2. Add winter melon pieces and salt. Stir for 1 minute.
3. Add water or soup stock, bringing to a boil. Turn heat down, cover, and cook winter melon for 5 minutes.
4. Using a tablespoon to scoop 1 tablespoon of the meatball mixture, make a round shape and drop into the soup pot one by one.

5. Cover and cook for 3–5 minutes or until meatballs are fully cooked and winter melon has softened.

6. Add white pepper powder and drop in sesame oil. Sprinkle green onion and cilantro on top. Remove and serve hot.

Winter melon, also called white gourd, ash gourd, "fuzzy gourd," or "fuzzy melon," is vine grown and prized for its very large fruit, eaten as a vegetable when matured. In Chinese cuisine, the melons are used in stir-fries, usually combined with pork bones/ribs or chicken to make winter melon soup.

Winter melon has a good amount of moisture along with a moderate composition of proteins, fiber, and carbohydrates. Therefore, it is often used in diets to reduce weight and excessive fat. Since it is low in calories, it is beneficial for diabetics and people who are trying to lose weight.

Sour Fish-Ball Soup

Ingredients

2 tablespoons cooking oil

1 teaspoon fresh minced ginger

1 teaspoon minced garlic

2 Chinese red chili peppers or jalapeños, deseeded and diced

1 cup tomato sauce

4 cups water

4 teaspoons sugar

¾ teaspoon salt for soup (or to taste) and 1 teaspoon for fish ball

4 pieces perilla or mint leaves

10 ounces tilapia fillet, rinsed and cut into small pieces

¼ box soft tofu, cut into small pieces

½ lemon, zested about 1 tablespoon

1 egg

2 teaspoons cornstarch

1 teaspoon white pepper powder or ½ teaspoon black pepper powder

1 cup bean sprouts, rinsed clean

Directions

1. Heat the wok, adding cooking oil, minced ginger, and garlic.

2. Add red chili peppers and tomato sauce. Stir for 3–4 minutes over medium heat.

3. Add water, sugar, salt, and two pieces of perilla. Bring to a boil, and then turn heat to low. Keep simmering.

4. Put tilapia and tofu pieces in a blender (ratio of fish to tofu is 2:1). Add 1 teaspoon of salt, lemon zest, egg, cornstarch, white pepper powder, and two pieces of perilla. Blend until sticky and smooth.

5. Scoop 1 tablespoon of the fish-tofu mixture and mold into a round shape. Carefully drop ball into the soup, one by one.

6. Bring soup back to a boil slowly on low to medium heat. Add bean sprouts. When fish balls float to the surface, squeeze some lemon juice into the soup. Remove and serve hot.

Perilla, like basil and coleus, is a member of the mint family. The overall plant resembles the stinging nettle, although the leaves are somewhat rounder. Traditionally used in Chinese medicine and cuisine, it has been shown to stimulate interferon activity and thus the body's immune system. It is often used to ease the symptoms of the common cold. Chinese weever is the preferred fish for this dish, though it is not commonly available outside of China. Tilapia is used as an option in this recipe.

Chinese red chili pepper is similar to jalapeño, but is spicier and smaller in size. If you cannot find the exact red chili pepper, feel free to use jalapeño or any chili pepper. Red color gives this dish a more appealing look.

Winter Melon with Shrimp Soup

Ingredients

10 medium-size shrimp, peeled and deveined

1 teaspoon cornstarch

½ teaspoon rice wine

2 teaspoons salt, divided, or to taste

1 tablespoon vegetable oil

3 slices fresh ginger

1 tablespoon green onion (scallions), chopped

10 ounces winter melon, peeled and deseeded, then cut into ½-inch thick and 1½-inch large pieces

3 cups soup stock

1 teaspoon white pepper powder or ½ teaspoon black pepper powder

2 teaspoons freshly chopped cilantro

Directions

1. Marinate shrimp in 1 teaspoon of cornstarch, ½ teaspoon of rice wine, and a pinch of salt.

2. Heat a soup pot or saucepan to medium-high heat. Add 1 tablespoon of vegetable oil. When hot enough, add ginger and green onion. Stir for 20 seconds.

3. Add winter melon. Stir for 1 minute. Add salt.

4. Add enough soup stock to cover winter melon. Bring to boil and turn heat down to keep it simmering.

5. When winter melon pieces turn tender, add shrimp.

6. When shrimp turns pink, sprinkle white pepper powder on top.

7. Toss in chopped cilantro before serving.

This soup is very light, healthy, and simple to make without sacrificing great taste. The combination of winter melon and shrimp is so delicious that you simply must try it (if you haven't already). Ham pieces can also be added for extra flavor and color.

Seafood Soup with Vegetables

Ingredients

2 cups water
2 cups chicken stock
10 clams, cleaned and cut in half
8 medium scallops, rinsed and cut into smaller pieces
½ box soft tofu, cut into small cubes
5 pieces baby corn, cut into small pieces
1 tablespoon sweet peas or green peas
1 stem celery, cut into small pieces

1 small carrot, peeled and cut into small pieces
1½ teaspoons salt, or to taste
1 teaspoon sugar
8 medium-size shrimp, shelled, deveined, and cut into small pieces
½ cup crabmeat
2 tablespoons cornstarch, mixed with 4 tablespoons water
1 egg white, slightly beaten
1 green onion (scallion), finely chopped

Directions

1. Add water and chicken stock in a soup pot. Bring to a boil.
2. Add clams and scallops to the soup.
3. Bring back to a boil. Turn heat down to continue simmering for 15 minutes.
4. Add tofu, baby corn, sweet pea, celery, carrot, salt, and sugar. Continue cooking for 5 minutes. Add shrimp and crabmeat, and continue cooking for 2 minutes.
5. Add cornstarch mixture, stirring gently until soup thickens.
6. Drop in egg white while stirring gently to make egg feather and spread.
7. Garnish with green onion. Serve hot.

This soup is very easy to make, while containing many nutritious ingredients. It is tasty and healthy, as well as being very colorful.

Meat & Poultry Entrées

Kung Pao Chicken

Ingredients

14 ounces chicken breasts (or legs), deboned and skinned
2 ⅔ tablespoons dark soy sauce
1 teaspoon salt, or to taste
1 teaspoon cooking wine
1 teaspoon cornstarch
1 teaspoon sugar
½ teaspoon vinegar
2 tablespoons cooking oil

2 teaspoons cornstarch, mixed with 1 tablespoon water
1 teaspoon Szechuan peppercorn
8 dried red chili
½ cup unsalted roasted peanuts
2 slices fresh ginger, cut into shreds
2 cloves garlic, sliced
1 green onion (scallion), chopped
½ teaspoon sesame oil

Directions

1. Cut chicken into bite size cubes. Marinate in mixture consisting of 2 teaspoons dark soy sauce, ¼ teaspoon of salt, 1 teaspoon of cooking wine and 1 teaspoon of cornstarch for 20–30 minutes.

2. In a small bowl, mix soy sauce, sugar, vinegar, salt, and cornstarch. Stir mixture well and set aside.

3. Heat wok over high heat, adding cooking oil. When hot, add peppercorn and dried red chilies.

4. When chilies and peppercorn turn darker, add ginger and garlic; stir for 20 seconds.

5. Add chicken pieces; stir-fry for 2 minutes or until chicken is completely cooked.

6. Pour in sauce mixture. Stir and coat meat well.

7. Add roasted peanuts and chopped green onions. Mix all ingredients well.

8. Garnish with sesame oil.

Kung pao flavor, a classic in Szechuan cuisine, is very popular in Chinese restaurants. It is characterized by its spiciness, which comes from the combination of dried chili and peppercorn. Kung pao flavor can be used to spice up anything from meat to vegetables to tofu.

This dish can be made either spicy or mild according to how much peppercorn and chili sauce is added, and both have their own unique flavor.

Chicken leg meat is tender, and is always preferred in authentic kung pao chicken cooking.

Kung Pao Chicken with Celtuce (Chinese Lettuce)

Ingredients

12 ounces boneless, skinless chicken breast or leg
1 teaspoon cornstarch
1 teaspoon cooking wine
1 teaspoon dark soy sauce
¾ teaspoon salt
½ carrot, peeled and cut into matching cubes
1 teaspoon sugar
2 teaspoons cornstarch, mixed with 1 tablespoon water
1 tablespoon soy sauce

¼ teaspoon rice vinegar
2 tablespoons cooking oil
8 dried red chilies
½ teaspoon Szechuan peppercorn
1 teaspoon minced ginger
2 cloves garlic, sliced
½ celtuce (Chinese lettuce root), peeled, cut, and cubed
1 green onion (scallion), chopped
⅓ cup roasted peanuts

Directions

1. Marinate chicken in mixture of 1 teaspoon of cornstarch, 1 teaspoon of cooking wine, 1 teaspoon of dark soy sauce, and ¼ teaspoon of salt for 15 minutes. Cut into bite-size cubes.

2. Add water in a saucepan and bring to a boil. Add carrots, cooking for 3 minutes.

3. In a small bowl, combine sugar, salt, cornstarch mixture, soy sauce, and vinegar. Mix well and set aside.

4. Heat the wok over high heat. Add cooking oil; when hot, add dried chilies and peppercorn.

5. When chili peppers turn darker, add ginger and garlic. Stir for 10 seconds.

6. Add chicken; stir-fry for 2 minutes or until meat is almost cooked.

7. Add carrots and Chinese lettuce root cubes. Stir for 2 minutes.

8. Add sauce mixture and green onion. Stir until sauce thickens, then add roasted peanuts and mixing well.

9. Place on a serving plate.

Traditionally, kung pao chicken is cooked with celtuce for its crispy and refreshing texture. Other than celtuce, vegetables like celery, carrots, bamboo shoots, green peas, and bell peppers are all good alternatives.

Celtuce (also called stem lettuce, celery lettuce, asparagus lettuce, or Chinese lettuce) is a cultivar of lettuce grown primarily for its thick stem and is used as a vegetable. It is especially popular in China.

Kung Pao Chicken with Snow Peas and Bamboo Shoots

Ingredients

14 ounces boneless, skinless chicken breast (or leg)

2 teaspoons dark soy sauce

1 teaspoon salt, or to taste

1 teaspoon cooking wine

1 tablespoon cornstarch

2 tablespoons light soy sauce

1 teaspoon sugar

½ teaspoon vinegar

20 snow peas, trimmed

½ cup cubed winter bamboo shoots or any bamboo shoots

2 tablespoons cooking oil

1 teaspoon Szechuan peppercorn

8 dried red chilies

2 slices fresh ginger, cut into shreds

2 cloves garlic, sliced

½ cup unsalted roasted peanuts

1 green onion (scallion), chopped

½ teaspoon sesame oil

Directions

1. Marinate chicken in 2 teaspoons of dark soy sauce, ¼ teaspoon of salt, 1 teaspoon of cooking wine, and 1 teaspoon of cornstarch for 20–30 minutes. Cut into bite-size cubes.

2. In a small bowl, mix light soy sauce, sugar, vinegar, salt, and cornstarch. Stir well and set aside.

3. Fill a saucepan half-full with water and bring to a boil. Add snow peas and bamboo-shoot cubes. Bring water to a boil again, cook for 45 seconds, and then drain.

4. Heat a wok to high heat. Add cooking oil; when hot, turn heat to medium-high, adding peppercorn and dried red chilies.

5. When chilies and peppercorn turn darker (do not burn), add ginger and garlic, and stir for 20 seconds.

6. Add chicken pieces, and stir-fry for 2 minutes or until meat turns white.

7. Add snow peas and bamboo shoots, and stir for 1 minute.

8. Pour in cornstarch mixture, and stir and coat meat well.

9. Add roasted peanuts and chopped onion. Mix well with the sauce.

10. Sprinkle with sesame oil and serve.

To make tasty and crispy peanuts, soak raw peanuts in hot water for 5 minutes, and then remove the skin. Heat the wok with 1 cup of oil. Heat oil to low heat, add peanuts, and stir frequently until peanuts turn a light golden brown. Drain and cool.

Steamed Chicken with Straw Mushrooms

Ingredients

4 organic chicken legs

15 dried straw mushrooms or shiikate mushrooms

1 teaspoon cooking oil

1 tablespoon dark soy sauce

1 green onion (scallion), cut into 1½-inch long sections

4 slices fresh ginger

1 teaspoon sugar

2 teaspoons cooking wine

1½ teaspoons cornstarch, mixed with 2 teaspoons water

1 teaspoon salt, or to taste

Directions

1. Trim off excess fat from chicken legs. Debone and cut into bite-size pieces.
2. Soak mushrooms in warm water for 30–45 minutes or until softened, rinse clean, and cut into quarters.
3. Combine chicken leg pieces with mushrooms and all seasonings. Mix well and marinate for 15 minutes.
4. Place in a heatproof ceramic bowl.
5. Add water in a steamer and bring to a boil.
6. Place the chicken bowl in the steamer on high heat and boil for 35–45 minutes.

The straw mushroom (also called "paddy straw mushroom") is available in canned and dried forms. Canned mushrooms can be purchased in Asian markets, while dried mushrooms can be found in Chinese herbal outlets. The latter has a more intense flavor than those found in cans.

Straw mushroom is high in fiber and protein. This dish, cooked with simple seasonings, tastes delicious, tender, smooth, and fresh. It is a healthy choice because it is low in sodium and oil. It can help to lower cholesterol and is especially beneficial for people with diabetes.

Steamed Orange Chicken

Ingredients

8 straw mushrooms
2 cups bite-size cubed chicken
breast
1 teaspoon rice cooking wine
1 tablespoon light soy sauce
1 teaspoon salt
1 teaspoon white pepper powder
or ½ black pepper powder

1 tablespoon chopped green onion (scallions)
2 teaspoons minced fresh ginger
1 teaspoon sesame oil
2 teaspoons cornstarch, mixed
with enough water to dissolve
4 medium-size oranges

Directions

1. Wash and rinse the straw mushrooms. Soak in warm water for 30 minutes or until soft, then rinse and cut into small pieces.

2. Combine chicken-breast cubes with mushrooms and all seasonings (except for the oranges). Mix well and marinate for 20 minutes.

3. Clean the oranges. Carve a cap into the orange peel. Take out the cap and remove the orange pulp. The orange shell will be used in this dish.

4. Divide chicken into four portions, putting one portion into each orange shell.

5. Bring water in a steamer to a boil; place the orange shells in the steamer. Steam for 40 minutes on medium-high heat.

Dry-Fried Chicken

Ingredients

2 tablespoons cooking oil

8 dried hot red chilies

1 teaspoon Szechuan pepper-corns

1 pound chicken breast, cut into bite-size chunks

1 clove garlic, minced

1 tablespoon chili-bean paste

3 teaspoons rice cooking wine

1 teaspoon dark soy sauce

2 stalks celery, outer layer peeled and cut in half in steep-angle pieces

1 piece winter bamboo shoot or any bamboo shoot, cut into thin slices (optional)

2 green onions (scallions), cut into 2-inch long sections

½ teaspoon sesame oil

¼ teaspoon salt, or to taste

Directions

1. Heat wok over high heat, adding oil; when hot, add dried red chilies and Szechuan peppercorn.

2. When chilies start to turn dark, add chicken chunks. Stir-fry for 4–5 minutes or until chicken has lost much of its water.

3. Turn the heat to medium-high, add minced garlic and chili-bean paste, and keep stirring until oil turns red.

4. Add rice wine and soy sauce; stir until chicken looks dry and fragrance is brought out (about 5–10 minutes).

5. Add celery, bamboo shoot, and green onion, and stir about 1–2 minutes or until celery turns tender but still crispy.

6. Garnish with sesame oil and place on a serving plate.

Dry-frying is one of the cooking techniques commonly used in Szechuan cuisine. The general idea is to cook your main ingredient—whether it's a protein (typically beef, chicken, or pork) or a vegetable (like long beans, green beans, or Chinese broccoli)—in a moderately hot oil without coating. As it cooks, the intense heat drives off interior moisture, thereby concentrating the flavor. Simultaneously, the exterior becomes dry and browned. After this dry-fry stage, foods are then very briefly stir-fried with a small amount of strongly aromatic ingredients. Chicken meat in this dish slowly takes on the flavors of the chilies and peppercorn in the cooking process. The result is intensely flavored food with a uniquely chewy, crisp texture.

Celery is a good balance for this dish with its flavorful yet crispy texture.

If the chili-bean paste you have on hand is salted, reduce the salt called for in this recipe. Bean paste can easily stick to the bottom of the pan. To avoid this, stir constantly and adjust heat level if necessary.

Stir-Fried Chicken with Sweet-Flour Sauce

Ingredients

1 pound boneless, skinless chicken breast, cut into bite-size cubes

1 egg

1 teaspoon soy sauce

1 teaspoon cornstarch

½ teaspoon salt, or to taste

3 tablespoons cooking oil

1 teaspoon minced ginger

2 tablespoons sweet-flour sauce or plum sauce

2 teaspoons cooking wine

2 teaspoons sugar

1 tablespoon water

3 green onions (scallions), halved and cut into 2-inch-long sections

½ teaspoon sesame oil

Directions

1. In a bowl, combine chicken, egg, soy sauce, cornstarch, and salt, mixing everything well.

2. Heat the wok. Add 2 tablespoons of cooking oil; when hot, add ginger and stir for 10 seconds.

3. Add chicken cubes. Stir-fry until chicken meat is almost done, and then remove and set aside.

4. Turn heat to low. Add remaining oil in the wok. Add sweet-flour sauce, cooking wine, sugar, and water. Stir quickly until sauce becomes sticky.

5. Turn heat to medium-high, add chicken and green onion sections, stir quickly, and evenly coat meat pieces with the sauce.

6. Garnish with sesame oil. Place on a serving plate.

Sweet-flour paste or sauce can be found in the seasoning/sauce section in many Asian grocery stores. A common replacement can be plum sauce.

Chicken with Bamboo Shoots

Ingredients

12 ounces chicken breast, cut into thin slices

1 egg white

1 teaspoon salt, or to taste

2 teaspoons cornstarch

5 dried black wood-ear mushrooms

20 snow peas, ends trimmed

1 piece winter bamboo shoot, rinsed and cut into thin slices

1 teaspoon sugar

2 teaspoons rice cooking wine

2 tablespoons chicken stock

2 tablespoons cooking oil

1 teaspoon thinly shredded ginger

½ teaspoon sesame oil

Directions

1. Cut chicken breast into thin slices and combine with egg white, ⅓ teaspoon of salt, and 1 teaspoon of cornstarch. Mix well and set aside.

2. Soak mushrooms in warm water for 40 minutes, tear into small pieces.

3. Blanch snow peas in boiling water until half-cooked. Blanch bamboo-shoot slices and black wood-ear mushrooms briefly.

4. In a small bowl, add sugar, salt, cornstarch, cooking wine, and chicken stock. Mix well and set aside.

5. Heat the wok over high heat. Add cooking oil; when hot, add ginger shreds, stirring for 10 seconds. Then add chicken, quickly stir-frying for 3–4 minutes or until almost done.

6. Add snow peas, black wood-ear mushrooms, and bamboo shoots. Stir for 1 minute.

7. Add sauce mixture and quickly stir coat everything well.

8. Garnish with sesame oil; place on a serving plate.

Fresh bamboo shoots can be hard to get. Frozen ones are equally tasty and are available in most Asian supermarkets. Thaw before cutting and cooking.

Sweet and Sour Chicken with Vegetables

Ingredients

1 tablespoon white rice vinegar or any rice vinegar

4 tablespoons sugar

½ teaspoon salt, or to taste

¼ teaspoon pepper

2 tablespoons cornstarch

½ cup water

2 ⅓ tablespoons cooking oil

1 stalk celery

1 cup Chinese cabbage, chopped

1 small onion, diced

1 carrot, shredded

¼ yellow bell pepper, diced

¼ red-green pepper, diced

1 teaspoon minced ginger

1 clove garlic, minced

12 ounces chicken breast, thinly sliced

½ cup tomato sauce

Directions

1. In a small bowl, mix vinegar, sugar, salt, pepper, cornstarch, and water, making sure to dissolve cornstarch well.

2. In a wok, add ½ teaspoon of cooking oil. Heat until hot and add all vegetables. Stir-fry until ingredients are cooked but still crispy. Remove and set aside.

3. Add 1½ tablespoons of oil to the wok; when hot, add ginger and garlic. Stir for 20 seconds, then add chicken and stir-fry until color changes to white (about 3–5 minutes).

4. Add ½ tablespoon of oil in the wok. Heat until hot, then turn heat to medium-high. Add tomato sauce, stirring for 2 minutes. Add sauce mixture (stir the mixture before pouring) and stir slowly.

5. When sauce starts to thicken, turn heat to high, add chicken back to the wok, and stir for 3 more minutes, coating chicken with the sauce.

6. Add vegetables. Stir and mix well.

7. Place on a serving plate.

Fish-Flavor Minced Chicken

Ingredients

12 ounces chicken breast

¾ teaspoon salt, or to taste

2½ teaspoons cornstarch

1 tablespoon dark soy sauce

1 tablespoon vinegar

1½ tablespoons sugar

2 teaspoons cooking wine

2 tablespoons cooking oil

1 tablespoon chili sauce

2 teaspoons minced ginger

1 tablespoon minced garlic

½ green bell pepper, cut into matching size of chicken

2 teaspoons chopped green onion (scallions)

Directions

1. Marinate chicken with mixture of ¼ teaspoon of salt and ½ teaspoon of cornstarch for 15 minutes. Cut the chicken into very small pieces (about the size of a soybean).

2. In a small bowl, combine soy sauce, vinegar, sugar, cooking wine, salt, and cornstarch. Mix well and set aside.

3. Heat the wok until hot, adding oil when heated. Add chicken and stir for 2 minutes or until chicken pieces are well separated.

4. Add chili sauce, ginger, and garlic. Stir for 3 minutes until chili sauce is well-cooked and fragrance is brought out.

5. Add bell pepper and mix with the chicken.

6. Add sauce mixture, stirring until sauce thickens.

7. Garnish with chopped green onion. Place on a serving plate.

Some chili sauce is salted; test and adjust total salt usage to taste.

Poached Chicken with Dipping Sauce

Ingredients

Dipping sauce
4 tablespoons soy sauce
½ teaspoon salt, or to taste
1 teaspoon sugar
2 tablespoons chicken stock
1 teaspoon sesame oil
1 teaspoon Szechuan peppercorn oil
1 green onion (scallion), finely chopped
1½ tablespoons cooking oil
1 tablespoon minced fresh ginger
Chili oil, to taste (optional)

Chicken
1 whole chicken (about 3 pounds, organic preferred)
Ice water, enough to cover the whole chicken
3 large slices fresh ginger
2 green onions (scallions), cut into sections
1 tablespoon cooking wine

Directions

Dipping sauce

1. In a small bowl, combine soy sauce, salt, sugar, chicken stock, sesame oil, Szechuan peppercorn oil, and chili oil. Mix well, and add chopped green onion on top.
2. Heat the wok over high heat. Add cooking oil; when hot, add ginger. Turn off the heat and immediately pour oil directly into the sauce mixture.
3. Mix well. Set aside for dipping.

Chicken

1. Rinse chicken clean and remove excess fat.
2. Add water (enough to cover the whole chicken) in a large stockpot. Bring water to a boil; add ginger slices, green onion sections, and cooking wine.
3. Slowly add the chicken, breast-side up. Bring water to a boil again. Turn heat to medium-low and cook for 10 minutes.
4. Cover the pot, turn off the heat, and leave the chicken in the pot for 15–20 minutes.
5. Insert chopsticks into the thickest part of the chicken's thigh. If no more juice comes out, it is done.
6. Slowly remove the chicken and place in ice water. Soak for 15 minutes or until chicken is cool. Drain.
7. After completely cooled and the chicken skin is dry, place chicken onto cutting board. Hop the chicken into large strips using a meat cleaver.
8. Place chopped chicken on a serving plate and serve with the dipping sauce.

This is a Cantonese-style dish. The chicken's skin will remain lightly colored (nearly white), and the meat will be quite tender, moist, and flavorful.

Chicken with Mushroom and Fresh Broad Beans

Ingredients

8 ounces boneless, skinless chicken breast
1 tablespoon cooking wine
1 teaspoon salt, or to taste
1 egg white
4 teaspoons cornstarch
1 teaspoon sugar
2 teaspoons light soy sauce

1 tablespoon water
1 cup fresh broad bean or Chinese green peas
2 tablespoons cooking oil
1 teaspoon minced ginger
10 fresh white mushrooms, cut into quarters
1 tablespoon oyster sauce
¼ teaspoon sesame oil

Directions

1. Remove excess fat from the chicken and cut into bite-size cubes. Mix well with 2 teaspoons of cooking wine, ½ teaspoon of salt, 1 egg white, and 2 teaspoons of cornstarch.

2. In a small bowl, combine sugar, soy sauce, salt, cooking wine, cornstarch, and water; mixing well.

3. Boil some water in a saucepan, add ¼ teaspoon of salt and all the broad beans. Cook for 6–7 minutes, drain, and set aside.

4. Heat the wok over high heat. Add cooking oil and minced ginger; stir for 10 seconds.

5. Add chicken pieces; stir-fry for 2–3 minutes or until meat turns white.

6. Add mushroom pieces and broad beans. Stir for 2 minutes.

7. Add oyster sauce; stir to mix. Add sauce mixture, stir until thickened, and mix well with all ingredients.

8. Garnish with sesame oil. Remove and place on a serving plate.

Broad bean is a member of the legume family. Fresh broad bean should be in pods and must be fully cooked before eating (boiling is an important procedure). Some people are sensitive and even allergic to them if they are not fully cooked. Boiling with a little salt will also help keep the color fresh.

Chinese green peas, while appearing similar to the green pea in most grocery stores, contain less liquid and have no sweet taste. It is a good replacement for broad bean and can be found in many Asian grocery stores, either as fresh or as frozen in the frozen-food section.

Chicken with Walnut and Soybean Paste

Ingredients

10 ounces boneless, skinless
chicken breast

2 teaspoons minced ginger

3 tablespoons cooking oil

2 tablespoons soybean paste or
sweet-flour sauce

2 teaspoons cooking wine

2 teaspoons sugar

½ cup roasted walnut

½ teaspoon sesame oil

Directions

1. Remove excess fat from chicken and cut into small bite-size cubes.

2. Soak ginger in 2 tablespoons of warm water for 5 minutes. Remove ginger, as only the ginger juice will be used in cooking.

3. Heat the wok over high heat, adding 2 tablespoons of cooking oil, and heat until hot.

4. Turn heat to medium. Add chicken cubes, stirring occasionally until meat turns white. Stir-fry for 2 more minutes. Remove and set aside.

5. Add 1 tablespoon of cooking oil in the wok; reheat the wok on medium-high heat.

6. Add soybean paste, ginger juice, cooking wine, and sugar. Stir slowly for 2 minutes to mix well (adjust heat if necessary to avoid burning).

7. Add chicken and walnut pieces; stir and coat well with the sauce.

8. Sprinkle sesame oil on top.

9. Remove and place on a serving plate. Serve hot.

This is a traditional Shandong-style dish. Soybean paste can be purchased from Asian supermarkets. If a sweeter flavor is desired, sweet-flour sauce can be substituted.

Raw walnut can be used directly in this dish for better nutritional value. Roasted walnuts are crispier and have more flavor. If you don't have roasted walnuts, you can fry them with oil on low heat until crispy.

Steamed Beef with Roasted Ground Rice

Ingredients

2 tablespoons cooking oil

2 tablespoons Szechuan chili–broad bean paste, finely chopped

1 teaspoon ground Szechuan peppercorn

1 star anise, torn into smaller pieces

2 teaspoons minced ginger

1 green onion (scallion), chopped

2 tablespoons soy sauce

2 teaspoons sugar

1 teaspoon salt

½ cup water

1 tablespoon rice cooking wine

½ teaspoon sesame oil

1 pound lean beef, cut across the grain into thin shreds

1 cup ground roasted rice (see next page)

1 tablespoon chopped cilantro

Directions

1. Heat the wok over high heat. Add cooking oil; when hot, turn heat to medium, add bean paste, peppercorn, star anise, ginger, and green onion. Stir-fry until oil becomes red.

2. Add soy sauce, sugar, salt, water, cooking wine, and sesame oil. Mix well. Place in a small bowl and allow to cool.

3. Place the beef shreds in a large bowl and add the sauce mixture. Marinate the beef for 30 minutes.

4. Add ground rice to the beef. Mix and coat every piece well.

5. Place the beef bowl in a steamer; steam over medium heat for 45–60 minutes.

6. Sprinkle the chopped cilantro on top and serve.

As beef has a tough texture, steaming time may be longer than indicated.

Ground roasted rice (also known as rice powder) can be purchased in Asian supermarkets. Making it yourself is also very easy by following the recipe on the next page.

Roasted Ground Rice

Ingredients

2 cups rice
1 star anise
2 teaspoons Szechuan peppercorn

Directions

1. Heat the wok over medium-high heat. Add all ingredients.

2. Turn heat to medium-low; toss slowly for 20 minutes or until rice turns golden brown (keep tossing; otherwise, the rice on the bottom will burn).

3. Put everything in a blender. Blend until all ingredients are coarsely ground (do not grind the rice too finely).

4. Let cool; use 1 cup for one recipe and put the rest in storage for next time.

Beef with Broccoli

Ingredients

12 ounces lean beef
½ egg
½ teaspoon salt
2 teaspoons cooking wine
1 tablespoon cornstarch
2 ⅓ tablespoons cooking oil
½ pound broccoli crowns, cut into bite-size pieces

2 cloves garlic, sliced
1 tablespoon light soy sauce
2 tablespoons oyster sauce
2 teaspoons sugar
1 tablespoon cornstarch, mixed with ¼ teaspoon salt and 2 tablespoons water
Few drops sesame oil

Directions

1. Cut beef across the grain into thin, bite-size slices. Mix well with ½ egg, ½ teaspoon of salt, 2 teaspoons of cooking wine, 1 tablespoon of cornstarch, and 1 teaspoon of cooking oil. Marinate for 30 minutes.

2. Boil water in a saucepan. Add broccoli and boil for 45 seconds to 1 minute (do not overcook); drain well.

3. Heat wok over high heat. Add oil and heat until hot; add garlic slices and stir for 20 seconds.

4. Add beef slices. Stir to separate pieces, then stir-fry until nearly cooked.

5. Add broccoli. Mix together with beef slices.

6. Add soy sauce, oyster sauce, and sugar. Stir to mix well.

7. Add cornstarch mixture, stir until thickened, and mix well with other ingredients.

8. Place on a serving plate and sprinkle sesame oil on top. Serve hot.

For vegetable lovers, you can add thinly sliced carrots and onion pieces. Boil carrots with broccoli as instructed.

Hunan Beef

Ingredients

12 ounces beef tenderloin
2 tablespoons soy sauce
1 tablespoon Chinese rice cooking wine
½ teaspoon salt
1 tablespoon cornstarch

2 tablespoons Chinese black vinegar or any dark-color vinegar
2 teaspoons sugar
2 cups broccoli crowns
2 tablespoons cooking oil
2 teaspoons minced garlic
5 dried red chilies
½ teaspoon sesame oil

Directions

1. Slice tenderloin thinly across the grain. Marinate with 1 tablespoon of soy sauce, 1 tablespoon of Chinese rice wine, ½ teaspoon of salt, and 2 teaspoons of cornstarch for 15 minutes.

2. In a small bowl, mix vinegar, soy sauce, cooking wine, sugar, and cornstarch together well, and set aside.

3. Boil water in a saucepan. Add broccoli crowns; boil for 1 minute, then drain well.

4. Heat the wok over high heat. When hot, add oil, garlic, and dried chilies. Stir until chilies turn a dark color.

5. Add beef slices; quickly stir-fry until no longer pink (about 1–2 minutes).

6. Add broccoli and stir-fry for another minute.

7. Add sauce mixture; keep stirring until sauce thickens. Mix everything and coat well.

8. Garnish with sesame oil and place on a serving plate.

Dry-Fried Shredded Beef

Ingredients

2 tablespoons cooking oil

2 teaspoons Szechuan peppercorns

3 dried red chilies, torn into smaller pieces

1 thumb-size piece ginger, finely shredded

1 pound lean beefsteak (sirloin), cut into long and thin strips across the grain

1 tablespoon chili-bean sauce or paste

1 tablespoon Chinese cooking wine or any cooking wine

½ teaspoon sugar

1 teaspoon soy sauce

2 stems celery, cut into shreds

1 small red bell pepper, cut into shreds

1 teaspoon ground Szechuan peppercorn

Directions

1. Heat oil in wok; add Szechuan peppercorn and dried chilies. Stir-fry until chilies turn a dark color. Remove chilies and peppercorns (can be added back later for an extra spicy flavor).

2. Turn heat to high. Add ginger shreds and beef, and spread the shreds with chopsticks or a spatula.

5. Keep stir-frying until beef is dark brown and dry. You need to keep stirring; otherwise, the meat on the bottom will burn (adjust heat level if necessary).

3. Push the meat to one side of the wok. Turn heat to medium-high, add chili-bean sauce/paste, and stir until oil is tinted a red color.

4. Turn heat to high again. Mix beef shreds and bean sauce well, adding cooking wine, sugar, and soy sauce.

5. Add celery and red pepper shreds. Stir-fry until vegetables are softened but still crispy.

6. Spread ground Szechuan peppercorn on top and place on a serving plate.

Dry-fried shredded beef is a traditional and delicious Szechuan dish. The fried meat is stir-fried first to make it dry, and then stir-fried a second time to give it a spicy and savory flavor. The meat is quite chewy, but very tasty. The rich, spicy flavor comes from the combination of dried chili, chili-bean sauce, and Szechuan peppercorn. The crispy celery gives it a good balance and adds a nice flavor to this meat dish.

Most chili-bean (broad bean) sauces are salted, so no extra salt is needed in this recipe.

Beef shreds will easily stick to the bottom of the wok and burn, so using a nonstick wok will be easier to handle.

Beef and Bell Pepper with Black Bean Sauce

Ingredients

8 ounces lean beef
1 teaspoon soy sauce
1 teaspoon rice wine
1 teaspoon sugar
1 teaspoon cornstarch
¼ teaspoon salt
1 teaspoon minced ginger
2 tablespoons cooking oil

½ green bell pepper, cut into small cubes
1 tablespoon fermented black bean, coarsely crushed
½ red bell pepper, cut into small cubes
Drops sesame oil

Directions

1. Cut beef into very thin slices across the grain. Marinate with 1 teaspoon of soy sauce, 1 teaspoon of rice wine, 1 teaspoon of sugar, 1 teaspoon of cornstarch, ¼ teaspoon of salt, and 1 teaspoon of minced ginger.

2. Heat the wok over medium-high heat. Add 1 teaspoon of oil.

3. Add green bell pepper cubes and stir until 80 percent cooked. Remove and set aside.

4. Reheat the wok over high heat, adding the remaining cooking oil.

5. Add beef slices. Stir quickly and separate pieces completely.

6. When color changes, add black beans while continuing to stir in order to mix with beef slices.

7. Add red bell pepper cubes and stir for another minute.

8. Remove from heat and place on a serving plate. Sprinkle sesame oil on top.

Fermented black bean, also called preserved black bean, is a type of fermented and salted soybean, known in Chinese as douchi. It is made by fermenting and salting black soybeans. The process turns the beans black, soft, and mostly dry. The aroma is sharp, pungent, and spicy in smell, with a taste that is salty and somewhat bitter and sweet. They are most widely used for making black bean sauce. It can be found in many Asian grocery stores.

Sliced Beef in Hot-Chili Oil

Ingredients

12 ounces beef tenderloin

½ teaspoon salt

1 teaspoon soy sauce

2 teaspoons cooking wine

4 teaspoons cornstarch, mixed with 2 tablespoons water

5 tablespoons cooking oil

1 teaspoon whole Szechuan peppercorn

2 teaspoons minced ginger

2 tablespoons chili sauce

2 green onions (scallions), cut into sections

1 celtuce (Chinese lettuce), peeled and cut into slices

2 cups hot water

1 cup mung bean sprouts

1 tablespoon ground chili

1 teaspoon Szechuan peppercorn powder

½ teaspoon sesame oil

Salt, to taste

Directions

1. Cut beef tenderloin into thin, bite-size slices across the grain. Marinate with ½ teaspoon of salt, 1 teaspoon of soy sauce, 2 teaspoons of cooking wine, and 4 teaspoons of wet cornstarch. Mix very well and make sure beef slices are well-coated.

2. Heat the wok over high heat. Add 3 tablespoons of cooking oil.

3. Add whole Szechuan peppercorn and ginger. Stir for 20 seconds, then adding chili sauce; stir on medium heat until oil is tinted with chili color.

4. Add green onion sections, Chinese lettuce slices, and hot water.

5. Bring water to a boil again, adding bean sprouts. Cook for 1 minute, and then remove all ingredients to a big serving bowl.

6. Turn heat to medium, adding beef slices one by one.

7. When all beef slices are put in the wok, turn heat to high, cover the wok, and cook for 2 minutes. Pour everything into the bowl.

8. Reheat the wok again, adding the remaining cooking oil. Turn heat to medium-high; add ground chili and stir-fry for 30–40 seconds (do not burn).

9. Add ground Szechuan peppercorn on top of the beef, and then pour the hot-chili oil directly over the peppercorn powder. Sprinkle with sesame oil and serve.

Some chili sauce is salted; taste and adjust as needed. Chili can be reduced based on taste.

This dish is rich in taste and bright in color, highlighting the unique spicy flavor of Szechuan cuisine. The beef tastes fresh, tender and smooth, while the vegetables give it a more balanced nutritional value with its uniquely fresh and crispy texture.

One of the representative dishes in Szechuan Cuisine, sliced beef in hot-chili oil is a very popular dish among the Chinese. Different from usual stir-fried dishes, this cooking method cooks meat in the chili soup. In Chinese, this dish is called "Water-Cooked Beef," and is basically cooked with water, although it is rich in oil. Other than beef, fish and pork are also commonly used meats. It usually comes with vegetables; bean sprouts, celery, Chinese cabbage (bok choy), Shanghai cabbage, and Chinese lettuce are among the most popular.

Traditionally, this dish is cooked in heavy oil; for the purpose of staying healthy, the amount of cooking oil has been significantly reduced in this recipe.

Beef with Oyster Sauce

Ingredients

14 ounces beef sirloin
½ egg
3 teaspoons cornstarch
4 teaspoons soy sauce
½ teaspoon salt
2 teaspoons sugar
6½ teaspoons cooking oil
½ teaspoon baking soda
5 slices fresh ginger

2 green onions (scallions), cut into sections
2 tablespoons water
2 teaspoons cooking wine
2 tablespoons oyster sauce
1 teaspoon white pepper powder
3 teaspoons cornstarch, mixed with 2 tablespoons water
2 stems cilantro, chopped
½ teaspoon sesame oil

Directions

1. Cut beef sirloin across the grain into very thin bite-size slices. Mix well with ½ egg, 3 teaspoons of cornstarch, 2 teaspoons of soy sauce, ½ teaspoon of salt, 1 teaspoon of sugar, ½ teaspoon of cooking oil, ½ teaspoon of baking soda, and let marinate for 1 hour.

2. Boil water in a saucepan over medium-high heat. Add beef slices, cook until color changes, remove, and drain well (stir very slowly to separate pieces, and do not use high heat).

3. Heat the wok over medium-high heat; add cooking oil and heat until hot. Add ginger slices and green onion sections, stirring for 20 seconds.

4. Add water, cooking wine, oyster sauce, 2 teaspoons of soy sauce, pepper powder, and sugar.

5. Bring to a boil.

6. Add beef slices and stir for 1–2 minutes. Add cornstarch mixture, stirring until thickened and fully coated.

7. Spread chopped cilantro on top and garnish with sesame oil. Remove and place on the serving plate.

This is a double-cook method for maintaining the tenderness of the beef slices. Traditionally, this effect is accomplished through deep-frying. However, boiling is easier for home-kitchen preparation and is also much healthier.

Shandong-Style Pork

Ingredients

12 ounces pork tenderloin, sliced

1 tablespoon cooking wine

1 teaspoon salt

½ teaspoon white pepper powder or ¼ teaspoon black pepper powder

1 egg white, slightly beaten

1 cup plus 4 teaspoons cornstarch, divided

¾ cup water

1 teaspoon plus 2 cups cooking oil, divided

2 teaspoons minced ginger

1 teaspoon minced garlic

1 tablespoon chopped green onion (scallions)

1 tablespoon vinegar

3 teaspoons sugar

2 teaspoons soy sauce

¼ teaspoon sesame oil

Directions

1. Marinate pork slices with 1 teaspoon of cooking wine, ½ teaspoon of salt, and ½ teaspoon of white pepper powder for 15 minutes. Cut into bite-size thin slices.

2. In a bowl, combine egg white, 1 cup of cornstarch, and ½ cup of water. Mix and stir until it turns into a thick and sticky batter. Add 1 teaspoon of cooking oil and mix well with the batter.

3. Mix pork slices with the batter, making sure all meat slices are evenly coated.

4. In a small bowl, mix 4 teaspoons of cornstarch with ¼ cup water.

5. Heat the wok over medium-high heat. Add 2 cups of cooking oil (or enough to deep-fry the pork slices). When oil is medium-hot, put pork slices into the wok piece by piece.

6. Fry for 5 minutes or until meat is set and almost cooked; remove all pieces from the wok.

7. Turn heat to high. Fry all pork slices for another 3 minutes or until coating turns crispy and golden brown. Remove and drain well using a colander.

8. Leaving 1 tablespoon of oil in the wok, and add ginger, garlic, and green onion. Stir for 20 seconds, and then add vinegar, 2 teaspoons of cooking wine, sugar, soy sauce, and ½ teaspoon of salt. Stir for 20 seconds, and then add cornstarch mixture, quickly stirring to thicken the sauce.

9. Add fried pork slices. Stir and coat all slices with sauce well.

10. Sprinkle sesame oil on top. Place on a serving plate.

This is a traditional Shandong-style pork recipe. Slightly sweet and sour in taste, this dish is characterized by its crispy coating and tender meat.

To balance the meat, vegetables such as carrots, celery, or snow peas can be added. Carrots (cut into thin slices) and snow peas need to be blanched in boiling water first.

When making the batter, add water slowly, making sure not to add too much water. The batter needs to be thick and sticky.

To reduce the amount of oil in the finished dish, use paper towels to absorb some of the oil before serving.

Fish-Flavor Shredded Pork

Ingredients

10 ounces lean pork

⅔ teaspoon salt, or to taste

1⅔ tablespoons soy sauce

1 tablespoon cooking wine

1 tablespoon cornstarch

⅓ cup shredded black wood-ear mushrooms

1 tablespoon vinegar (Chinese black vinegar preferred)

3 teaspoons sugar

1 carrot, peeled and cut into thin shreds

½ cup shredded winter bamboo shoots or any bamboo shoots

1 small piece fresh ginger, cut into thin shreds

2 tablespoons cooking oil

3 cloves garlic, minced

1 tablespoon chili sauce

2 green onions (scallions), cut into shreds

Directions

1. Cut pork into thin shreds. Marinate with ⅓ teaspoon of salt, 2 teaspoons of soy sauce, 2 teaspoons of cooking wine, and 1 teaspoon of cornstarch for 15 minutes.

2. Soak the dried black wood-ear mushrooms in warm water for 30 minutes or until softened. Rinse and cut.

3. In a small bowl, combine soy sauce, vinegar, sugar, salt, cooking wine, and cornstarch. Stir and mix well.

4. Boil water in a saucepan and blanch carrot shreds and bamboo shreds briefly.

5. Heat wok until hot over medium-high heat and add cooking oil.

6. Add ginger, garlic, and chili sauce. Stir for 30 seconds or until oil is tinted with red color and fragrance is brought out.

7. Turn heat to high, add pork shreds, and quickly stir-fry (separate shreds completely). Stir for 2 minutes or until meat is almost cooked.

8. Add carrots, bamboo shoots, and black wood-ear mushroom shreds. Stir for 1 minute.

9. Pour in sauce mixture; quickly stir until thickened and all ingredients are mixed well.

10. Remove and place on a serving plate. Garnish with green onion shreds on top.

A traditional and well-loved recipe, this is an eye-catching, colorful dish that tastes sweet, sour, salty, fresh, and delicious.

As with all Chinese fish-flavor dishes, it has a rich, fresh, and fragrant fish flavor, but does not contain fish or fish sauce. The flavor comes from the combination of chili sauce, sugar, vinegar, garlic, and ginger.

Chicken, beef, tofu, and eggplant can all be cooked using this same method.

If a darker color is preferred, you can use dark soy sauce.

Some chili sauce is salted, so be sure to taste and adjust salt as needed.

The authentic way of making this dish is to use pickled red chili, which should be finely chopped.

Diced Beef with Crispy Garlic

Ingredients

12 ounces beef tenderloin

1 egg white

2 tablespoons potato starch

½ teaspoon salt

1 teaspoon cooking wine

10 large cloves garlic

3 tablespoons cooking oil

1 tablespoon chili sauce

1 green onion (scallion), cut into sections

1 teaspoon white pepper powder or ½ teaspoon black pepper powder

Directions

1. Cut beef tenderloin into small cubes. Mix well with 1 egg white, 2 tablespoons of potato starch, ½ teaspoon of salt, and 1 teaspoon of cooking wine.

2. Cut garlic into thick slices. Soak in cold water, and then briefly blanch with boiling water, drain, and set aside.

3. Heat oil in the wok on low-medium. Add garlic slices, stir-fry until golden brown and crispy; then remove and set aside.

4. Add marinated beef cubes. Fry lightly golden brown and crispy; remove.

5. Add chili sauce, stir until fragrant, and add green onion sections, beef, pepper powder, and garlic. Stir and quickly mix well.

6. Remove and place on a serving plate. Serve hot.

This dish is a typical example of Shandong-style cuisine. Tasting slightly spicy, the beef is crispy outside and tender inside. The crispy garlic is delicious and serves to enhance the flavor of the beef.

Potato starch is preferred; it gives the beef a crispy crust while maintaining the beef's tenderness.

Sweet-Flour Sauce Pork

Ingredients

12 ounces lean pork (pork tenderloin)

1 teaspoon cooking wine

½ teaspoon salt

2 tablespoons cooking oil

1 small piece fresh ginger, cut into thin shreds

1½ tablespoons sweet-flour paste/sauce

½ cup shredded winter bamboo shoots

Directions

1. Cut pork into thin shreds and marinate with 1 teaspoon of cooking wine and ½ teaspoon of salt for 15 minutes.
2. Heat the wok until hot over high heat; add cooking oil.
3. Add ginger shreds, stirring for 20 seconds.
4. Add pork shreds, stir-frying for 2–3 minutes until all shreds are separated completely and almost cooked.
5. Turn heat to medium and add sweet-flour sauce. Stir and mix until pork shreds are well-coated.
6. Add bamboo shreds. Stir for 1 minute, add green onion, and stir to mix well. Remove and place on a serving plate. Serve hot.

A traditional Beijing-style dish characterized by its appealing color and delicious taste, it is an easy-to-prepare homemade dish.

The sweet-flour sauce can be easily burned, and as a result, will taste bitter, so adjust heat if necessary.

In many of these recipes, pork can be replaced with boneless and skinless chicken breast or leg meat. If eating red meat is a health concern, simply replace pork with chicken. They are equally delicious and tasty.

Pork with Tomato Sauce

Ingredients

12 ounces lean pork (tenderloin)
¾ teaspoon salt
1 teaspoon cooking wine
1 egg
2½ tablespoons cooking oil
1 green onion (scallion), cut into sections
1 teaspoon minced ginger

3 tablespoons tomato sauce
⅓ cup water
1½ tablespoons sugar
2½ teaspoons Chinese vinegar or any vinegar
2 teaspoons cornstarch, mixed with 1 tablespoon water

Directions

1. Cut pork into bite-size thin slices. Mix with ¼ teaspoon of salt, 1 teaspoon of cooking wine, and 1 egg, and marinate for 15 minutes.
2. Heat the wok over high heat and add 2 tablespoons of cooking oil.
3. Add pork slices; stir-fry until 80 percent cooked and remove from the wok.
4. Add remaining cooking oil, green onions, and ginger. Stir-fry for 20 seconds.
5. Turn heat to medium, add tomato sauce, and stir for 50 seconds.
6. Add water, salt, sugar, and vinegar; stir and bring to a boil.
7. Add pork slices, cooking for 1 minute.
8. Add cornstarch mixture, and stir and thicken the sauce. Place on a serving plate and serve.

This is a Shandong-style dish, characterized by its slightly sweet and sour flavor and appealing bright color (white rice vinegar is preferred for maintaining the color).

Shredded Pork with Green Peppers

Ingredients

10 ounces lean pork
½ egg
½ teaspoon salt
1 teaspoon dark soy sauce
1 teaspoon cooking wine
1 teaspoon cornstarch
2 tablespoons cooking oil
1 teaspoon minced ginger

5 Chinese green peppers, shredded
½ teaspoon vinegar
½ granulated chicken bouillon cube
½ teaspoon sugar
3 green onions (scallions), green part removed and white part cut into shreds
¼ teaspoon sesame oil

Directions

1. Cut pork into fine shreds. Marinate with ½ egg, ¼ teaspoon of salt, 1 teaspoon of dark soy sauce, 1 teaspoon of cooking wine, and 1 teaspoon of cornstarch. Mix with chopsticks until very sticky.

2. Heat the wok over high heat and add cooking oil.

3. Add minced ginger; stir for 10 seconds.

4. Add pork shreds, stir-fry until completely separated and color changes (2–3 minutes or about 70–80 percent cooked).

5. Add green-pepper shreds, stirring for 1–2 minutes.

6. Add salt, vinegar, chicken bouillon, and sugar; stir to mix well. Add green onion shreds.

7. Stir quickly and sprinkle sesame oil on top. Place on a serving plate.

Chinese green pepper, different from bell pepper, is spicier and smaller in size, which can be found in many Asian grocery stores. If you cannot find Chinese green peppers, jalapeños are a good replacement.

Pork with Cashews

Ingredients

12 ounces lean pork
4 teaspoons cornstarch
½ teaspoon salt, or to taste
1 teaspoon cooking wine
½ egg white
2 teaspoons minced ginger

1 green onion (scallion), cut into sections
1 teaspoon sugar
2 tablespoons water
1 teaspoon soy sauce
2 tablespoons cooking oil
1 clove garlic, cut into slices
½ cup roasted cashews

Directions

1. Cut pork into small cubes. Mix well with 2 teaspoons of cornstarch, ⅓ teaspoon of salt, 1 teaspoon of cooking wine, and ½ egg white.

2. In a small bowl, combine minced ginger, chopped green onion, cornstarch, sugar, water, and soy sauce. Mix well.

3. Heat the wok over high heat, adding cooking oil.

4. Add garlic slices; stir for 5 seconds.

5. Add pork cubes; stir quickly for 2–3 minutes or until meat is fully cooked.

6. Add sauce mixture; stir until sauce thickens.

7. Add cashews. Stir and mix all ingredients well, and place on a serving plate.

This Shandong-style dish is delicious and simple to cook. It is characterized by the contrast between the tenderness of the meat and the crispiness of the cashews. Vegetables such as snow peas and bell peppers can also be added to this dish for a more balanced nutritional value.

Pork with Vegetables and Walnuts

Ingredients

8 ounces lean pork
¾ teaspoon salt
2 teaspoons cooking wine
2 teaspoons light soy sauce
2 teaspoons cornstarch
2½ tablespoons cooking oil
2 teaspoons minced ginger
1 green onion (scallion), chopped
⅓ cup winter bamboo, cut into small cubes

2 ounces dried tofu, cut into small cubes
2 tablespoons chicken stock or water
¼ red bell pepper, cut into cubes
¼ green bell pepper, cut into cubes
2 teaspoons sugar
3 teaspoons cornstarch, mixed with 2 tablespoons water
⅓ cup roasted walnut

Directions

1. Cut pork into small cubes. Mix well with ¼ teaspoon of salt, 1 teaspoon of cooking wine, 2 teaspoons of light soy sauce, and 2 teaspoons of cornstarch.
2. Heat the wok, adding 2 tablespoons of cooking oil. Add ginger and green onion, and stir for 20 seconds.
3. Add pork cubes; stir-fry until cooked. Remove and set aside.
4. Add remaining cooking oil. Add bamboo shoots, dried tofu, and chicken stock (or water). Cook for 1–2 minutes; then add pepper cubes and stir-fry for 40 seconds.
5. Add pork cubes back to the wok; add sugar, salt, and cooking wine.
6. Add cornstarch mixture and stir until thickened.
7. Remove and place in a serving plate. Put walnut on top.

If you don't have roasted walnuts, you can fry walnuts in oil over low heat until crispy (high heat will overcook or burn the walnuts, which will result in a bitter taste).

Pork Spareribs Steamed with Lotus Leaf

Ingredients

2 pounds pork spareribs

1 cup sweet (sticky) rice

1 fresh lotus leaf or dried bamboo leaf

1½ teaspoons salt

1 tablespoon cooking wine

2 teaspoons white pepper powder

2 tablespoons dark soy sauce

2 teaspoons minced ginger

1 tablespoon chopped green onion (scallions)

2 tablespoons peanut butter

1 tablespoon cooking oil

Directions

1. Cut spareribs into bite-size pieces. Clean, drain, and place in a large bowl.
2. Soak sweet rice in warm water for 1 hour and drain.
3. Soak lotus leaf in cold water with some salt for 30 minutes; rinse clean.
4. Combine spareribs with 1½ teaspoons of salt, 1 tablespoon of cooking wine, 2 teaspoons of white pepper powder, 2 tablespoons of dark soy sauce, 2 teaspoons of minced ginger, 1 tablespoon of chopped green onion, and 2 tablespoons of peanut butter.
5. Mix all ingredients very well with hands.
6. Add sweet/sticky rice. Mix well with spareribs and marinate for 30 minutes.
7. Add water in the steamer, bring to a boil, and lay lotus leaf flat in the steamer.
8. Put marinated spareribs on the lotus leaf.
9. Steam for 50–60 minutes over medium-high heat.
10. Remove and place steamed spareribs on a serving plate.

11. Sprinkle chopped green onion on top.
12. Heat cooking oil in the wok until hot and pour directly over chopped green onion.

For this recipe, you can also use dried lotus leaf, which is easier to find in Asian supermarkets. Soak dried lotus leaf in warm water for 1 hour to soften it. If you can't get either fresh or dried lotus leaf, dried bamboo leaf is also a good option (soak in warm water for 2 hours).

Ready-to-cook spareribs are also available in most Asian supermarkets.

Cooked in this way, spareribs and sticky rice are tender and tasty, with the lotus leaf lending it a fresh fragrance. This is a very easy dish to prepare and is well-loved in Chinese cuisine.

Triple Delight

Ingredients

1 teaspoon salt, divided
1 teaspoon light soy sauce
1 teaspoon sugar
3 tablespoons water
1 granulated chicken bouillon cube
4 teaspoons cornstarch, divided
2 teaspoons cooking wine
1 egg white

15 snow peas
2 ounces winter bamboo shoots, cut into thin slices
1 ounce dried black wood-ear mushrooms
2 tablespoons cooking oil
1 clove garlic, minced
1 teaspoon minced ginger
10 ounces lean pork, sliced
¼ teaspoon sesame oil

Directions

1. In a small bowl, combine salt, soy sauce, sugar, water, chicken bouillon, and cornstarch. Mix well.

2. Boil some water in a saucepan. Add snow peas; cook for 1 minute. Blanch bamboo and black wood-ear mushrooms briefly. Remove and set aside.

3. Heat the wok over high heat. Add cooking oil, garlic, and ginger; stir for 20 seconds.

4. Add pork slices and stir-fry for 2–3 minutes or until almost cooked. Add snow peas, bamboo-shoot slices, and black wood-ear mushrooms, quickly stirring for 1 minute.

5. Add sauce mixture, stirring until thickened. Mix all ingredients well and sprinkle sesame oil on top.

6. Remove and place in a serving plate.

Lamb Slices with Scallions

Ingredients

12 ounces boneless lamb leg meat
½ teaspoon salt
2 teaspoons dark soy sauce
1 teaspoon sugar
2 teaspoons cooking wine
2 teaspoons wet cornstarch
½ teaspoon sesame oil

½ teaspoon white pepper powder
or black pepper powder
2 tablespoons cooking oil
1 tablespoon thinly shredded
ginger
5 green onions (scallions), cut
diagonally into 1½-inch long
sections

Directions

1. Trim off excess fat from lamb. Cut into thin slices and marinate in ½ teaspoon of salt, 2 teaspoons of dark soy sauce, 1 teaspoon of sugar, 2 teaspoons of cooking wine, 2 teaspoons of wet cornstarch, ½ teaspoon of sesame oil, and ½ teaspoon of white pepper powder. Mix well and set aside.

2. Heat the wok over high heat, adding cooking oil. Add ginger shreds and stir for 20 seconds.

3. Add lamb slices. Quickly stir and separate pieces completely.

4. When color changes, add green onion and stir quickly for 1 minute.

5. Remove from heat and place on a serving plate.

This recipe sounds simple and easy; however, cooking it successfully can be a challenge. It requires the whole process to be finished quickly over very high heat to maintain the tenderness and freshness of the meat.

As an alternative for green onion, a medium-size onion can be used. In this case, the onion needs to be cut into smaller pieces and precooked until it is 70 percent done.

Lamb with Cumin

Ingredients

12 ounces boneless lamb (leg or shoulder meat)

2 teaspoons cooking wine

2 teaspoons dark soy sauce

½ teaspoon salt

2 tablespoons cooking oil

1 teaspoon minced garlic

1 teaspoon minced ginger

1 teaspoon crushed red chili flakes

2 teaspoons ground cumin

5 stems cilantro, cut into small pieces

Directions

1. Trim off excess fat from lamb and cut into thin slices. Marinate with 2 teaspoons of cooking wine, 2 teaspoons of dark soy sauce, and ½ teaspoons of salt for 15 minutes.

2. Heat the wok over medium-high heat. Add cooking oil and heat until hot.

3. Add garlic, ginger, and chili flakes. Stir for 20 seconds.

4. Turn heat to high. Add lamb slices, quickly stirring until meat separates completely.

5. When color darkens, add ground cumin. Stir and mix well.

6. Add cilantro pieces. Stir quickly.

7. Remove and place on a serving plate.

The whole process for this recipe requires a quick finish over high heat to maintain the tenderness and freshness of the meat.

Ingredients like cumin, green onion (scallions), onion, or garlic are always used in cooking lamb meat to enhance and balance the meat flavor.

Seafood Entrées

Shrimp with Pepper-Salt

Ingredients

¼ cup lemon juice

4 teaspoons light soy sauce

½ teaspoon sesame oil

½ teaspoon sugar

3 cups cabbage (preferably Napa), thinly sliced

1 small red bell pepper, cut into thin shreds

1 small orange bell pepper, cut into thin shreds

¼ cup cornstarch

½ teaspoon salt

1 teaspoon freshly ground pepper

1 teaspoon Szechuan peppercorn powder

20 large raw shrimp, peeled and deveined

3 tablespoons cooking oil

2 jalapeño peppers, deseeded and diced

Directions

1. Whisk lemon juice, soy sauce, sesame oil, and sugar in a large bowl until the sugar is dissolved. Add cabbage and bell peppers; toss and mix well.

2. In a bowl, mix cornstarch, salt, pepper, and Szechuan peppercorn powder. Add shrimp and coat evenly with the spice mixture.

3. Heat oil in a wok over medium-high heat. When hot, add shrimp. Stir gently and fry for about 3–4 minutes until shrimp turns pink and curls up and coating becomes crispy.

4. Add jalapeños and fry for another minute.

5. Toss on top of the slaw and serve.

Szechuan peppercorn powder can be replaced by five-spice powder, which can be found in the spice section of most Asian supermarkets. There are many versions for this recipe, with most using Szechuan peppercorns. Five-spice powder is a good option, as it already contains Szechuan peppercorns and is more readily available.

Spice-crusted stir-fried shrimp with a cool, crisp Asian-style slaw is an easy dish. Cornstarch can be replaced by rice flour, which is made from finely milled white rice.

Chinese Broccoli Shrimp with Black Bean Sauce

Ingredients

8 ounces Chinese broccoli (kai-lan)

2 tablespoons rice cooking wine

2 teaspoons light soy sauce

2 teaspoons cornstarch

1 teaspoon sugar

1 tablespoon water

Pinch salt

1 tablespoon cooking oil

1 small piece peeled fresh ginger, very thinly shredded

2 cloves garlic, sliced

½ jalapeño chili, deseeded and cut into shreds

2 tablespoons fermented black bean, chopped

1 pound large raw shrimp (about 25), shelled and deveined

¼ teaspoon sesame oil

Directions

1. Trim broccoli and peel stalks, halving any thick stalks. Cut into 2½-inch long pieces, separating leafy parts from stems.

2. Mix rice wine, soy sauce, cornstarch, sugar, water, and salt in a small bowl.

3. Bring water to boil in a large saucepan, adding stems to boil for 2 minutes. Add leafy parts for 2 minutes or until tender. Drain very well and place on a serving plate.

4. Heat wok over high heat. Add oil and heat until hot, turning heat to medium and adding ginger, garlic, and jalapeño. Stir for 10 seconds, add chopped black bean, and stir for another 20 seconds.

5. Add shrimp as a layer on the bottom of the wok. Cook undisturbed for 3 minutes, then stir-fry until shrimp turns pink on both sides.

6. Stir in sauce mixture. Bring to boil and stir for another minute.

7. Sprinkle sesame oil on top.

8. Place shrimp on top.

Chinese broccoli, also known as kai-lan, is the Cantonese name for a leafy vegetable featuring thick, flat, glossy blue-green leaves with thick stems and a small number of tiny, almost vestigial flower heads similar to those of broccoli. Kai-lan is eaten widely in Chinese cuisine and especially in Cantonese cuisine. Common preparations include kai-lan stir-fried with ginger and garlic, and boiled or steamed and served with oyster sauce.

Stir-Fried Shrimp with Cashews

Ingredients

1 tablespoon rice wine
1 egg white, lightly beaten
1½ tablespoons cornstarch
½ teaspoon salt, or to taste
¼ teaspoon ground pepper
½ teaspoon minced ginger

1 pound small shrimp, shelled
and deveined
2 tablespoons cooking oil
¼ cup unsalted cashew nuts
2 green onions (scallions),
chopped

Directions

1. Mix ½ tablespoon of wine, 1 egg white, 1 tablespoon of cornstarch, salt, pepper, and ginger in a bowl to make a smooth batter. Add shrimp and toss gently to coat thoroughly. Set aside.
2. Mix remaining wine and cornstarch in a small bowl.
3. Heat oil to medium-hot in a wok with low heat. Add cashews and fry. Stir and fry until crispy. Remove and set aside.
4. Add shrimp to stir-fry for about 3 minutes or until crispy.
5. Add green onions and cornstarch mixture. Stir until sauce thickens.
6. Stir the cashews back into the wok; mix with shrimp.
7. Remove and place on a serving plate.

Stir-Fried Salmon with Eggs

Ingredients

4 slices salmon fillets (about 2 ounces each), cut into thin strips

2 tablespoons cornstarch

2 teaspoons sugar

1 tablespoon rice vinegar

1 tablespoon light soy sauce

1 teaspoon cooking wine

1 teaspoon salt, or to taste

3 tablespoons cooking oil, for stir-frying

1 tablespoon green onion (scallions), finely chopped

2 teaspoons freshly minced ginger

2 large eggs, beaten, plus pinch salt

½ carrot, peeled and thinly shredded

Directions

1. Marinate salmon strips with cornstarch, sugar, vinegar, soy sauce, wine, and salt in a bowl.

2. Heat wok over high heat. When hot, turn to medium-high and add 3 tablespoons of cooking oil.

3. Add green onion and ginger; stir for 30 seconds.

4. Add salmon strips; gently stir until color changes.

5. Add egg and scramble until set. Stir and mix well.

6. Place on a serving plate, garnishing with carrot shreds.

This egg and salmon stir-fry recipe is a great example of how egg really enhances the flavor of a salmon dish. It is very simple to make and tastes delicious.

Shrimp with Garlic Sauce

Ingredients

25 medium-size shrimp, shelled and deveined

3 teaspoons cornstarch

2 teaspoons rice cooking wine

¼ teaspoon salt, or to taste

5 dried black wood-ear mushrooms

1½ tablespoons water

1 tablespoon dark rice vinegar

3 teaspoons soy sauce

1 tablespoon sugar

1 tablespoon fresh ginger, minced

3 cloves garlic, minced

½ cup winter bamboo shoots, shredded

2 tablespoons hot-chili sauce/paste

2 tablespoons cooking oil

Directions

1. Marinate shrimp with 2 teaspoons of cornstarch, 2 teaspoons of rice cooking wine, and a pinch of salt for 15 minutes.

2. Soak black wood-ear mushrooms in warm water for 30 minutes or until softened, then shred.

3. Mix all seasonings (vinegar, soy sauce, sugar, ginger, and garlic) in a small bowl. Set aside for 1 hour. Stir occasionally to blend ingredients well.

4. Blanch bamboo shoots and black wood-ear mushrooms in a boiling saucepan. Drain well and set aside.

5. Heat wok until hot. Add cooking oil and, when hot, turn heat down to medium, add chili sauce, and stir for a minute.

6. Turn heat to high; add shrimp, quickly stirring.

7. When shrimp color changes to pink (1–2 minutes), add bamboo shreds and black wood-ear mushroom shreds. Stir for 30 seconds, and then pour in sauce mixture.

8. Stir for 1 minute to make sure sauce coats evenly.

If chili sauce paste is salted, there is no need for extra salt. If you are using pickled chili pepper (and if it is freshly chopped), add more salt to the sauce mixture.

Fried shrimp are commonly used in this dish in many Chinese restaurants. However, you'll find it is equally tasty and delicious (and healthier) by following this recipe.

Fish flavor, also known as garlic sauce in many Chinese restaurants, is one of the most popular flavors in Szechuan cuisine. No fish is used; the unique flavor comes from the mixture of ginger, garlic, vinegar, sugar, and chili sauce. You can use this sauce mixture to cook a large variety of meats, vegetables, and tofu.

Steamed Halibut with Ginger

Ingredients

1 pound halibut fillet
1 teaspoon kosher salt
1 small piece fresh ginger, thinly shredded or mined
2 green onions (scallions), thinly sliced

1 tablespoon dark soy sauce
2 tablespoons light soy sauce
1½ tablespoons peanut or other vegetable cooking oil
½ teaspoon sesame oil
6 fresh cilantro sprigs, chopped (optional)

Directions

1. Pat halibut dry with paper towels. Rub both sides of the fillet with salt.

2. Scatter the shredded or minced ginger over the top of the fish. Place in a heatproof dish or bowl.

3. Put water in a steamer and bring to a boil. Place the fish into the steamer; cover and steam for 10–12 minutes over medium heat.

4. Pour excess water out of the dish and sprinkle green onion on top. Drizzle soy sauces over.

5. Heat cooking oil and sesame oil in a wok over medium-high heat. When hot (beginning to smoke), carefully pour oil on top of the fillet. The hot oil will bring out the fragrance of the green onions.

6. Sprinkle cilantro on top and serve.

Five-Color Fish

Ingredients

½ pound tilapia fillet
1 teaspoon salt, divided
2 teaspoons cooking wine, divided
½ egg white
2 teaspoons wet cornstarch, divided
3 dried shiitake mushrooms

2 tablespoons water
½ cup green peas
½ cup sweet corn
½ red bell pepper, seeded and cut into small cubes
2 tablespoons cooking oil
2 teaspoons minced fresh ginger
1 green onion (scallion), chopped

Directions

1. Rinse tilapia and pat dry with paper towel. Cut into small cubes and mix well with ½ teaspoon of salt, 1 teaspoon of cooking wine, ½ an egg white, and 1 teaspoon of wet cornstarch.
2. Soak mushrooms in warm water for 45 minutes; rinse and cut into small pieces.
3. In a small bowl, combine water, salt, cornstarch, and cooking wine. Mix well.
4. Boil water in a saucepan. Cook green peas, sweet corn, bell pepper, and mushrooms separately until almost cooked. Drain well.
5. Boil marinated fish cubes in the same saucepan until 80 percent cooked. Do not stir. It is done when the meat turns white.
6. Heat the wok over high heat. Add cooking oil, ginger, and green onion; stir for 20 seconds.
7. Add fish cubes and all vegetables, and stir for 30 seconds.
8. Add sauce mixture. Quickly stir for 30 seconds or until everything is well-coated. Remove and place on a serving plate.

Steamed Perch

Ingredients

1 whole perch (1–1½ pounds)
2 green onions (scallions), cut into 2-inch long sections
10 thinly sliced pieces fresh ginger
1 tablespoon cooking wine

½ granulated chicken bouillon
1½ teaspoons salt
1 tablespoon cooking oil
3 cloves garlic, chopped
1 cup chopped red chili

Directions

1. Remove scales and innards from perch. Clean and score symmetrically on both sides. Place on a plate and set aside.

2. Marinate the fish with green onions, ginger slices, cooking wine, chicken bouillon, and 1 teaspoon of salt for 20 minutes.

3. Heat a wok until hot over high heat. Add cooking oil, garlic, chopped red chili, and remaining salt, and turn heat to medium-high. Stir-fry for 1 minute or until fragrance comes out.

4. Place the marinated fish in a heatproof dish. Lay a thin layer of the stir-fried chili mixture on the fish.

5. Put water in a steamer and bring to a boil. Place the fish plate in the steamer and steam for 10–12 minutes.

You can garnish this dish with shredded green onion before serving for a more appealing look.

This dish has a strong taste due to the spicy red chili, but is still rather tender and fresh. The combination of fish and red chili gives it a unique taste, and is a very popular dish in Hunan cuisine.

Perch is rich in a variety of nutrients. Its docosahexaenoic acid (DHA) is the highest among freshwater fish, so it is very helpful for enriching the brain. In addition, it also contains high-quality protein alongside a low fat content. Grass carp or carp are also good options.

Steamed Fish

Ingredients

1 whole perch (1–1½ pounds)
1 tablespoon rice cooking wine
1 teaspoon salt
2 green onions (scallions), cut
into 2-inch long sections and
shredded in half
2 teaspoons cooking oil

1 tablespoon light soy sauce
1 tablespoon fish sauce
2 teaspoons cornstarch, mixed
with 2 tablespoons water
1 piece (2½– by 1 inches) fresh
ginger, peeled, half cut into thin
slices and half into thin shreds

Directions

1. Remove scales and innards from fish. Clean and score it symmetrically on both sides. Place on a plate and set aside.
2. Place the fish in a heatproof plate. Marinate on both sides and inside with wine, ½ teaspoon of salt, green onion sections, and ginger slices for 20 minutes.
3. Put water in a steamer and bring to boil. Place the plate in the steamer and steam for 8–10 minutes. Turn off the heat and let the fish plate stay inside the steamer for another 5 minutes.
4. Heat a wok until hot over high heat. Add cooking oil, pour in the fish juice from the plate, and add soy sauce, fish sauce, salt, and the cornstarch mixture. Stir and mix to thicken the sauce.
5. Remove the green onion sections and ginger slices used for steaming and lay a thin layer of green onion shreds and ginger shreds on the fish.
6. Pour the stir-fried sauce onto the fish.

This is a lighter version of the Steamed Perch on page 168, an authentic and typical way of cooking fish in Chinese cuisine. The Chinese believe that cooking in this way will not only preserve the nutrition and original flavor of the fish, but will also fully bring out the freshness and tenderness of the fish.

Fish sauce, a sauce primarily used for cooking fish, can be found in the seasoning section in many Asian grocery stores.

Stir-Fried Fish with Vegetables

Ingredients

1 pound fresh fish fillets

1 teaspoon salt, divided

¼ teaspoon pepper

2 teaspoons rice wine, divided

1 egg white

1 ⅔ tablespoons cornstarch, divided

5 dried shiitake mushrooms

1 teaspoon sugar

5 tablespoons chicken stock

1 carrot, peeled and cut into shreds

15 snow peas

3 tablespoons cooking oil, divided

1 clove garlic, minced

1 tablespoon fresh ginger, cut into thin shreds

¼ red bell pepper, cut into shreds

1 green onion (scallion), chopped

¼ teaspoon sesame oil

Directions

1. Skin and shred fish fillets. Combine with ½ teaspoon of salt, ¼ teaspoon of pepper, 1 teaspoon of rice wine, 1 egg white, and 2 teaspoons of cornstarch. Mix well and marinate for 15 minutes.

2. Soak mushrooms in warm water for 40 minutes and shred.

3. In a small bowl, mix cornstarch, salt, cooking wine, sugar, and chicken stock, then set aside.

4. Blanch carrots and snow peas in boiling water until half-cooked. Drain well and set aside.

5. Heat a nonstick pan or wok over medium-high heat. Add 2 tablespoons of cooking oil, and when oil is moderately hot, add fish shreds. Panfry until light golden brown. Remove and set aside.

6. Add remaining cooking oil in the wok; when hot, add garlic and ginger, and stir for 15 seconds.

7. Add bell pepper and mushrooms; stir-fry for 1 minute, then add carrots and snow peas. Stir for another minute.

8. Add fish shreds and chopped onions; then add sauce mixture. Stir to coat everything well with the sauce.

9. Place in a serving plate, and sprinkle sesame oil on top.

This five-color dish is very appealing. Well-balanced with good protein and vegetables, it tastes delicious and fresh with tender fish and crispy vegetables.

Shrimp with Lobster Sauce

Ingredients

1 tablespoon preserved or fermented black beans

2 cloves garlic, minced

1 small piece fresh ginger, peeled and minced

1 tablespoon rice cooking wine

2 tablespoons vegetable oil

1 pound large shrimp, shelled, deveined, and butterflied

6 ounces ground pork

1 small onion, diced

1 green onion (scallion), chopped

½ green bell pepper, diced

½ teaspoon sugar

½ tablespoon light soy sauce

¾ cup chicken stock

1 tablespoon cornstarch, mixed with 2 tablespoons water

1 egg, lightly beaten with ¼ teaspoon salt

Dash white pepper powder

Several drops sesame oil

Directions

1. Put preserved black beans in a bowl. Add lukewarm water (enough to cover the beans) for 5 minutes and drain excess water.

2. Combine beans with minced garlic and ginger, and crush into a paste. Add wine and mix well. Set aside.

3. Heat the wok over medium-high heat. Add 1 tablespoon of oil; when hot, add shrimp and stir-fry for about 1–2 minutes. When shrimp begin to curl and turn pink, remove from the wok and put on a serving plate (keep warm).

4. Add remaining oil, heat until hot again over medium heat. Add black bean paste and stir for 10 seconds.

5. Add ground pork; stir-fry for about 3 minutes or until color changes.

6. Turn heat to high; add onions, peppers, sugar, and soy sauce. Mix and stir-fry until vegetables begin to soften (about 1 minute).

7. Add chicken stock, bring to a boil, and stir in the cornstarch mixture. Stir quickly to thicken.

8. Stir in the beaten egg. Sprinkle white pepper powder and sesame oil. Remove the sauce from the heat. Pour over shrimp and serve.

The sauce can be used with either shrimp or lobster. Be sure to add the egg just before serving the sauce.

Preserved black bean is also known as fermented black bean, which can be found in most Asian supermarkets.

Kung Pao Shrimp

Ingredients

1 pound small shrimp, shelled and deveined

3½ teaspoons cornstarch, divided

¾ teaspoon salt, divided, or to taste

1 teaspoon cooking wine

1 tablespoon light soy sauce

1 teaspoon sugar

1 teaspoon white rice vinegar or any rice vinegar

2 tablespoons chicken broth or water

2½ tablespoons cooking oil

6 dried red chili peppers

1 teaspoon minced ginger

2 cloves garlic, sliced

2 tablespoons chopped green onion (scallions)

½ cup roasted peanut

Directions

1. Marinate shrimp in 2 teaspoons of cornstarch, ¼ teaspoons of salt, and 1 teaspoon of cooking wine for 15 minutes.
2. In a small bowl, mix soy sauce, sugar, salt, cornstarch, vinegar, and chicken broth. Set aside.
3. Heat the wok over high heat. Add 2 tablespoons of oil and heat until hot. Add shrimp and stir-fry until shrimp turns pink and curls up (1–2 minutes). Remove and set aside.
4. Reheat the wok on medium-high heat, adding remaining oil and dried chili peppers. When peppers' color turns darker, add minced ginger and garlic. Stir for 30 seconds.
5. Add sauce mixture and quickly stir to thicken. Add shrimp back to the wok, adding chopped green onion.
6. Add peanuts, stir, and mix well with the sauce.
7. Place on a serving plate and serve.

This is a basic kung pao-flavor recipe. Many vegetables can be added to make this dish healthier. Green peas, bamboo shoots, diced celery and carrots, or Chinese lettuce are all good choices. Just make sure to boil or precook the vegetables, and add back to the wok with the shrimp when the sauce is ready.

Tofu Entrées

Braised Tofu

Ingredients

6 dried shiitake mushrooms
2 tablespoons vegetable oil
1 box medium or soft tofu, cut into big square pieces (10–12 pieces)
2 green onions (scallions), cut into 2-inch long sections
4 slices ginger
2 tablespoons frozen green peas

1 medium carrot, thinly sliced
3 teaspoons soy sauce
1 teaspoon sugar
½ cup water
½ granulated chicken bouillon cube
2 teaspoons cornstarch, mixed with 1 tablespoon water and ¼ teaspoon salt
½ teaspoon sesame oil

Directions

1. Soak mushrooms in warm water for 30 minutes or until softened, and cut into quarters.
2. Heat oil in wok until hot and fry tofu until golden brown. Remove and add green onions, ginger, and shiitake mushrooms. Stir for 10 seconds.
3. Add fried tofu, peas, carrots, soy sauce, sugar, water, and chicken bouillon. Cover and cook over medium heat until tofu absorbs the flavor.
4. Add cornstarch. Mix well.
5. Sprinkle sesame oil on top. Place on a serving plate.

Vegetarian Stir-Fried Dry Tofu

Ingredients

1 tablespoon cooking oil
1 stalk celery, cut into 2-inch long strips
1 medium carrot, cut into slices
½ medium-size onion, cut into small pieces
2 slices fresh ginger
1 green onion (scallion), cut into sections
½ package dry tofu, cut into thin slices

1 tablespoon light soy sauce
½ teaspoon salt, or to taste
2 teaspoons cornstarch, mixed with 1 tablespoon water
½ cup roasted peanuts or cashew nuts
½ teaspoon sesame oil
2 teaspoons spicy chili sauce (optional)

Directions

1. Heat 1 teaspoon of oil in wok to medium hot. Add vegetables and stir-fry until half-cooked. Remove and set aside.
2. Heat remaining oil in wok until hot. Add ginger and green onions, and stir for 20 seconds.
3. Add tofu. Stir for 1–2 minutes.
4. Add vegetables and stir-fry with tofu together for 2 minutes.
5. Add soy sauce, salt, and cornstarch. Stir until thickened, and then toss in peanuts.
6. Sprinkle sesame oil onto top.
7. Remove from wok and place on a serving plate.

Stir-Fried Dry Tofu with Bean Sprouts

Ingredients

1 tablespoon vegetable oil
2 cloves garlic, sliced
1 package dry tofu, cut into thin shreds
2 cups soy bean sprouts, washed
1 red chili pepper, shredded
½ teaspoon salt
½ teaspoon sugar
2 teaspoons soy sauce

Directions

1. Heat oil in wok until hot. Add garlic slices, turning heat down to medium-high. Add dry tofu shreds and stir for 2 minutes.
2. Add bean sprouts, red pepper shreds, salt, and sugar. Turn heat to high and stir-fry for 2 minutes.
3. Add soy sauce and mix well.
4. When bean sprouts turn soft, remove from the wok.
5. Place on a serving plate.

The bean sprouts in this dish taste fresh and crispy, while the tofu is chewy with a unique fragrance.

Braised Mushrooms and Tofu

Ingredients

2 tablespoons cooking oil
4 cloves garlic, minced
2 teaspoons ginger, minced
4 Portobello mushroom caps, cut into small pieces
1 tablespoon chili-garlic sauce or chili–broad bean paste
1 cup stock, mushroom broth, or water

2 teaspoons rice wine
2 tablespoons light soy sauce
1 teaspoon sugar
1 box (14 ounces) firm tofu
3 teaspoons cornstarch, mixed with 2 tablespoons water
1 teaspoon freshly ground Szechuan peppercorn

Directions

1. Heat oil in a saucepan or wok over medium heat. Add garlic and ginger, stirring until fragrant. Add mushrooms and chili-garlic sauce. Stir until most of the mushroom liquid has evaporated (3–5 minutes).

2. Add broth, rice wine, soy sauce, sugar, and tofu, and bring to boil. Turn the heat down but maintain a simmer. Cook for 4–5 minutes until flavors blend well.

3. Stir in the cornstarch mixture until the sauce is thickened (about 1 minute).

4. Sprinkle ground Szechuan peppercorn on top.

This is a vegetarian version of Mapo Tofu on page 184. Portobello mushrooms are used in this recipe instead of ground pork or beef.

Chili-garlic sauce (also called chili-garlic paste) is a mixture of ground chilies and garlic. It can be found in most Asian supermarkets. Chili–broad bean sauce can also be used. Most chili sauce or broad bean sauce is salted, so make sure to check before adding salt to this recipe.

Mapo Tofu

Ingredients

2 tablespoons ground pork or beef

2 teaspoons cooking rice wine

1 tablespoon soy sauce

1 box medium-firm tofu

2 tablespoons cooking oil

1 teaspoon fermented black beans, mashed

1 tablespoon chili–broad bean paste

½ cup water or chicken broth

2 green onions (scallions), coarsely chopped

1 tablespoon cornstarch, mixed with 1 tablespoon water and 2 tablespoons soy sauce

1 teaspoon freshly ground Szechuan peppercorn

Directions

1. Marinate meat with 2 teaspoons of cooking rice wine and 1 tablespoon of soy sauce for 20 minutes.
2. Cut tofu into cubes and blanch for 1–2 minutes in boiling water. Drain and set aside.
3. Heat wok with oil until hot. Turn heat to medium-high and add marinated pork. Stir-fry pork until the color darkens.
4. Add the fermented black beans, stirring until well-blended with the meat. Add chili–broad bean paste, stirring for 1 minute.
5. Add tofu and water.
6. Cook for 3–4 minutes until thoroughly heated.
7. Add green onions.
8. Add cornstarch mixture. Stir gently.
9. Sprinkle the ground Szechuan peppercorn on top.
10. Remove and place in a serving bowl.

This is a typical Szechuan-style dish, characterized by a combination of tofu set in a spicy chili-and-bean–based sauce—typically a thin, oily, bright-red liquid, and is often cooked with water chestnuts, onions, and other vegetables.

True Mapo tofu is powerfully spicy, with both conventional "heat" spiciness and the characteristic numbing spiciness of Szechuan cuisine. The feel of this particular dish is often described by cooks using several specific Chinese adjectives: numbing, spicy-hot, tender, and soft. The most important and necessary ingredients in this dish that give it this distinctive flavor are chili–broad bean paste, fermented black beans, and Szechuan peppercorns.

Broad bean paste is a spicy, salty paste made from fermented broad beans, soybeans, salt, rice, and various spices. It can be found in plain and spicy versions, with the latter containing red chili peppers. It is used particularly in Szechuan cuisine, and in fact, the people of the province commonly refer to it as "the soul of Szechuan cuisine." It can be found in many Asian grocery stores.

Home-Style Tofu

Ingredients

3 ounces lean pork, cut into thin shreds

1 teaspoon cornstarch

2 teaspoons soy sauce

2 teaspoons rice wine

Cooking oil, as needed to fry tofu chunks

1 box firm tofu, cut into triangular or diamond-shape chunks

1 tablespoon broad bean paste

20 snow peas

1 green pepper, cut into chunks

1 red chili pepper, cut into chunks

1 teaspoon sugar

2 teaspoons cornstarch, mixed with 2 tablespoons water

Directions

1. Cut pork into thin shreds and marinate with 1 teaspoon of cornstarch, 2 teaspoons of soy sauce, and 2 teaspoons of rice wine. Mix well.

2. Heat wok over high heat until hot, adding tofu chunks one by one. Fry over medium heat until tofu turns light brown. Drain and set aside.

3. Leaving 2 tablespoons of oil in the wok, add broad bean paste and stir for 20–30 seconds until fragrant.

4. Add marinated pork. Stir-fry for about 2 minutes until pork shreds are almost cooked.

5. Add snow peas and peppers. Stir for 2 minutes.

6. Add tofu pieces. Stir for 1 minute, and then add sugar and cornstarch mixture, mixing everything well.

7. Remove and place on a serving plate.

Winter bamboo shoots and carrots can also work well in this dish. This dish is red-gold in color and soft in texture.

Broad bean paste/sauce can be easily burned and will taste bitter, so adjust heat level when necessary.

Tofu with Garlic Sauce

Ingredients

1 box of firm tofu, cut into large pieces (about 12 pieces)

Cornstarch, as needed

Cooking oil, as needed

5 cloves garlic, cut into quarters

⅓ cup water

1½ tablespoons oyster sauce

½ teaspoon salt

2 teaspoons cornstarch, mixed with 1 tablespoon water

1 green onion (scallion), chopped

Directions

1. Coat tofu pieces individually with cornstarch powder.
2. Heat oil in a deep-frying pan and fry the tofu pieces until coating is light brown and crispy. Drain and set aside.
3. Leaving 1 tablespoon of oil in the wok, heat until hot and add garlic pieces until fragrant.
4. Add water, oyster sauce, and salt. Bring to a boil, and then add cornstarch mixture.
5. When sauce thickens, add tofu pieces. Mix and coat tofu well. Garnish with chopped green onions on top.

Oyster sauce can contain MSG, so if this is a concern, make sure to look for non-MSG options.

If you are vegetarian, you can find vegetarian oyster sauce in Asian supermarkets, made from mushrooms instead of oysters.

Clay-Pot Tofu

Ingredients

5 shiitake mushrooms
2 tablespoons oil for panfrying tofu, plus 1 tablespoon oil for cooking
1 box firm tofu (about 14 ounces), cut into triangular or diamond-shape chunks
1 tablespoon oil
2 cloves garlic, chopped
2 slices ginger

1 tablespoon light soy sauce
½ tablespoon oyster sauce
1½ cups water or chicken stock
15 snow peas
1 carrot, cut into thick slices
6–8 medium-size shrimp, shelled and deveined
1 green onion (scallion), chopped
Dash white pepper
½ teaspoon salt, or to taste

Directions

1. Soak mushrooms in warm water for 30 minutes and rinse.
2. Heat a nonstick pan or wok with 2 tablespoons cooking oil until hot, turn down to medium-high, and panfry tofu until light golden brown on both sides Remove and set aside.
3. Heat a large soup pan (a clay pot is preferred) and add 1 tablespoon of oil.
4. Add garlic and ginger until fragrant. Add mushrooms, soy sauce, oyster sauce, and water. Bring to a boil.
5. Add fried tofu, snow peas, and carrots. Bring back to boil. Cover the pot and turn heat to low to braise for 10 minutes.
6. Add shrimp. Cook for 2 minutes.
7. Toss in chopped green onions. Sprinkle white pepper onto top.

(see note on next page)

Shiitake mushrooms are a symbol of longevity in Asia. Due to their health-promoting properties, they have been used medicinally by the Chinese for more than 2,000 years. Clay pots add an earthy aroma to this dish and make the food a lot more appealing just because it's cooked and served in a clay pot.

This clay pot full of firm tofu with mushrooms is no exception. Decorated with blacks, greens, and reds with crispy yet tender shrimp, it is colorful, healthy, and delicious. In the winter, when the days are short and the nights are cold, a clay pot is like a fireplace: it gives you that warm, cozy feeling.

If you are using a clay pot, make sure not to add in cold water while cooking, as the difference in temperature may cause the clay pot to crack.

Kung Pao Tofu

Ingredients

2 teaspoons cornstarch
2 teaspoons water
½ teaspoon salt, or to taste
1 tablespoon soy sauce
1 teaspoon rice vinegar
2 teaspoons sugar
3½ tablespoons cooking oil
1 box firm tofu, cut into bite-size cubes

6 dried chili peppers
1 clove garlic, chopped
1 teaspoon minced ginger
6 ounces broccoli crowns, cut into bite-size pieces
¼ yellow bell pepper, diced
¼ red bell pepper, diced
2 tablespoons roasted peanuts
½ teaspoon sesame oil

Directions

1. Mix cornstarch well with water, salt, soy sauce, rice vinegar, and sugar in a small bowl and set aside.
2. Heat 3 tablespoons of cooking oil in a wok over medium-high heat. Add tofu and fry until light brown. Remove and set aside.
3. Add ½ tablespoon of oil in the wok, reheat, and add dried hot chili peppers. Stir until color turns darker. Add garlic and ginger to bring out the fragrance.
4. Add broccoli and yellow and red bell pepper, and stir until they begin to soften.
5. Add cornstarch mixture, stirring until thickened.
6. Add tofu and peanuts. Stir to coat well with the sauce.
7. Sprinkle sesame oil on top.

Tofu, along with many fresh vegetables, is stir-fried in this favorite Chinese dish. Traditionally, the tofu would not be deep-fried, as is so often the case in America. Other vegetables like celery and carrot also work well with this dish.

Spicy Tofu Flower

Ingredients

1 box of silken tofu
½ teaspoon salt
2 teaspoons light soy sauce
¼ teaspoon white pepper powder
or black pepper powder
1 tablespoon preserved pickle,
finely chopped

1 tablespoon finely chopped
green onion (scallions)
½ teaspoon sesame oil
2 teaspoons hot-chili oil
¼ Szechuan peppercorn powder
1 tablespoon roasted peanuts,
coarsely chopped

Directions

1. Add water to a saucepan and bring to a boil.
2. Add the box of silken tofu and cut into chunks with a ladle or spoon.
3. Bring to a boil again and remove to drain most of the water.
4. Place in a large serving bowl.
5. Mix all seasonings and ingredients (except peanuts) in a small bowl.
6. Pour over the boiled silken tofu chunks.
7. Stir roughly, toss in chopped peanuts, and serve.

This is a simple version of a traditional Spicy Tofu Flower recipe. It is soft, warm tofu covered with toppings that add crunch and flavor, often served as a popular side dish.

Tofu flower (douhua in Chinese) is a dish made with very soft tofu and can be sweetened or salted. Tofu flower in Szechuan is often made without any sugar, but with a number of condiments such as chili oil, soy sauce, Szechuan preserved pickle, Szechuan peppercorn, scallions, and nuts instead, and is sometimes eaten along with white rice.

Preserved pickle (zha cai in Chinese) is a type of pickled mustard-plant stem originating from Szechuan. The taste is a combination of spicy, sour, and salty, while the aroma is similar to sauerkraut with hot-chili paste. It can be found in many Asian grocery stores.

Fish-Flavor Tofu

Ingredients

10 dried black wood-ear mushrooms

1 piece winter bamboo shoot, cut into thin slices

2 tablespoons cooking oil, for panfrying tofu, plus 1 tablespoon for cooking

1 box firm tofu, evenly cut into thick slices (about 12–14 pieces)

2 tablespoons ground pork

2 teaspoons minced ginger

1 tablespoon minced garlic

1 chopped green onion (scallion)

1 teaspoon dark soy sauce

1 tablespoon red-chili paste

2 teaspoons cooking wine

1 tablespoon sugar

¾ teaspoon salt

1 teaspoon light soy sauce

1 tablespoon vinegar

1 teaspoon chili oil

1 tablespoon cornstarch, mixed with 3 tablespoons water

½ teaspoon sesame oil

Directions

1. Soak mushrooms in warm water for 40 minutes or until softened. Clean, remove roots, and tear into smaller pieces.

2. Boil water in a saucepan, cook winter bamboo shoot slices and black wood-ear mushrooms briefly, and drain.

3. Heat a nonstick pan or wok over high heat. Add 2 tablespoons cooking oil and arrange one layer of tofu pieces in the wok. Panfry both sides to a light golden brown and drain with a colander.

4. Add 1 tablespoon of cooking oil in the wok, reheating until hot over medium-high heat. Add ground pork, stirring until meat is well-cooked (about 2 minutes).

5. Add ginger, garlic, green onion, and dark soy sauce. Stir for 20 seconds.

6. Add chili paste. Stir for 1 minute, then add water and fried tofu pieces. Turn heat to medium and cook for 1–2 minutes.

7. Add cooking wine, sugar, salt, light soy sauce, 2 teaspoons of vinegar, and chili oil. Stir and cook for 1 minute.

8. Add cornstarch. Stir until sauce thickens and all ingredients are well-mixed. Add remaining vinegar, sprinkling sesame oil on top.

9. Remove and place on a serving plate. Serve hot.

Some chili sauce is salted, so be sure to taste and adjust salt usage accordingly.

Five-Color Tofu

Ingredients

2 dried Chinese mushrooms

1 cup water or stock

1 carrot, cut into cubes matching size of peas and corns

½ cup green peas

½ cup sweet corn

10 small-size shrimp, shelled and deveined

1 tablespoon cooking oil

2 teaspoons fresh minced ginger

1 box soft tofu, cut into small cubes

1 teaspoon salt, or to taste

½ granulated chicken bouillon cube

1 tablespoon cornstarch, mixed with 2 tablespoons water

Directions

1. Soak mushrooms in warm water for 35 minutes or until softened, and dice.
2. Add water in a saucepan and bring to a boil.
3. Add carrot and cook for 1 minute.
4. Add green peas, sweet corn, and mushrooms, and cook for 1 minute.
5. Add shrimp and bring water back to a boil.
6. Remove everything and drain well.
7. Add cooking oil in the heated wok, adding ginger to bring out the fragrance.
8. Add tofu and water. Bring to a boil.
9. Add precooked vegetables and shrimp. Add salt and chicken bouillon, stirring gently and cooking for 1–2 minutes.
10. Add cornstarch mixture to thicken the sauce.
11. Place on a serving plate.

A colorful, healthy, and easy-to-make tofu dish, this recipe serves as a good starting place when learning how to cook tofu.

Medicinal Foods

Winter Melon with Goji Berries (Wolfberries)

Ingredients

5 ounces pork ribs, excess fat trimmed off, cut into 2-inch-long sections, and parboiled

3 slices ginger

⅓ cup Chinese pearl barley (coix seeds), soaked for 25 minutes

1 pound winter melon, peeled and cut into ½– by 2-inch slices

1 tablespoon goji berries (wolfberries)

Salt, to taste

Directions

1. Bring water to a boil in a soup pot (preferably a clay pot). Add ribs, ginger slices, and barley. Turn heat to low, cover, and simmer for 1 hour.

2. Add winter melon and wolfberries. Simmer for another 25–30 minutes or until winter melon softens.

3. Add salt to taste. Turn off the heat; let soup stand for 10 minutes.

Winter melon can help to eliminate excess fluid in the body and is often used as a weight-loss aid. It is also good for regulating blood sugar.

Chinese pearl barley (coix seed) is a widely used ingredient. It is believed that coix seeds serve as a diuretic, as well as an antiswelling and cooling agent. It is therefore most commonly recommended to people suffering from stiff and painful joints, rheumatism, warts, and eczema. Barley also soothes the stomach, so it is beneficial if you have an easily irritable stomach.

This soup is light, so do not use too much salt.

Celery Congee

Ingredients

½ cup white rice
½ cup brown rice
6½ cups water
4 stems celery, cleaned and cut into bite size cubes
½ cup oatmeal
Salt, to taste
Pepper, to taste

Directions

1. Rinse white and brown rice.
2. Add water in a large pot or soup pot. Bring to a boil.
3. Add brown rice and white rice, bringing back to a boil again.
4. Turn heat to low. Simmer for 1 hour, stirring occasionally to avoid stickiness on the bottom.
5. Add celery and oatmeal. Keep simmering for another 30 minutes.
6. Add salt and pepper to taste.

Celery is often used in weight-loss diets, as it provides a large amount of low-calorie dietary fiber. Celery is often purported to be a "negative-calorie food," based on the assumption that it contains fewer calories than it takes to digest.

Shiitake Mushroom with White Gourd

Ingredients

2 teaspoons olive oil or vegetable oil

1 clove garlic, chopped

1 teaspoon green onion (scallions), chopped

10 shiitake mushrooms (if using dried mushrooms, soak in warm water for 30 minutes), torn into smaller pieces

½ pound white gourd or pumpkin, cut into small pieces

1 teaspoon light soy sauce

1 teaspoon oyster sauce

½ cup water

2 teaspoons cornstarch, mixed with 2 tablespoons water

Directions

1. Heat wok to medium heat. Add oil, garlic, and onion. Stir for 20 seconds.

2. Add mushroom and white-gourd pieces. Stir.

3. Add soy sauce, oyster sauce, and water. Cover and simmer for 10 minutes over medium heat or until gourd softens.

4. Add cornstarch mixture and stir evenly.

Although much of medicinal food is prepared as soup, there are a variety of other ways that food with curative properties can be prepared. Several of the recipes presented here are examples of this variety; this particular one can be served as a side dish at breakfast, lunch, or dinner. It is beneficial for people suffering from high blood pressure and high blood sugar. It is also suitable for people with diabetes.

Steamed Pumpkin with Rice

Ingredients

2 cups rice
1 pound pumpkin
1 teaspoon olive oil
½ teaspoon green onion (scallions), chopped
⅓ teaspoon salt

Directions

1. Rinse rice and soak in water for 30 minutes. Drain off most of the water and place in a bowl that can fit in a steamer.
2. Peel off pumpkin skin and remove seeds. Cut into ½-inch-thick cubes.
3. Put soaked rice in a steamer. Steam for 15 minutes (until half-cooked).
4. Heat oil in a wok. Add green onion, pumpkin, and salt. Stir for 1–2 minutes.
5. Add pumpkin pieces into the steamer. Continue to steam for 15–20 minutes.

This can be served as the main dish at lunch or dinner. It is tasty with fresh pumpkin and is beneficial for people with diabetes.

Ginseng and Chicken Soup

Ingredients

3 ounces ginseng

1 pound organic chicken breast, with skin and bone

6 cups water

3 slices fresh ginger

1 teaspoon coriander

1 teaspoon salt (optional)

1 teaspoon chopped green onion (scallions)

Directions

1. Rinse ginseng in water; cut it into smaller pieces if too large.
2. Trim off excess fat from the chicken.
3. Using a big soup pot (clay pot is preferred), add water and heat to boiling.
4. Add chicken, ginger, coriander, and ginseng into the pot.
5. Turn heat to low-medium and simmer for 2½ hours. Add salt and green onion for seasoning.
6. Serve the meat and soup together.

Ginseng is hailed by many as the "king of herbs," and is a very well-known Chinese ingredient in many recipes. Mild and nourishing in nature, ginseng can warm the body, regenerate energy, and strengthen the immune system. It is beneficial to people with hypertension and diabetes. It is also suitable for people with chronic diseases.

Chicken is a good source of carnosine, an antioxidant. The chicken and any vegetables used also provide much needed supplements to boost the immune system and nourish the body.

Mung Bean with Goji Berries and Astragalus

Ingredients

1 cup mung beans
1 tablespoon goji berries (wolfberries)
5 cups water
5 pieces astragalus root
½ cup rice

Directions

1. Rinse mung beans and goji berries. Put in a soup pot (preferably a clay pot). Add water.
2. Bring water to a boil. Turn heat to low and simmer for 45 minutes.
3. Add astragalus root; continue to cook for another 25 minutes.
4. Turn off the heat. Serve after short cooling period.

Astragalus is a root with a mild licorice-like taste. Modern research has proven that it possesses antiviral and anti-aging benefits, as well as myriad benefits for a wide range of illnesses, which is why it is featured frequently in Chinese tonic

Astragalus root can be found in stores carrying Chinese herbs in Chinatowns or can be ordered online.

This recipe is beneficial for those who are suffering high blood pressure and diarrhea.

Chicken with Goji Berries and Chinese Yam

Ingredients

½ small organic chicken or game hen

10 ounces Chinese yam (huai shan) or any yam

1 tablespoon goji berries (wolf-berries)

10 dried red dates

3 slices fresh ginger, sliced

2 teaspoons rice wine

½ teaspoon salt, or to taste

Directions

1. Clean the chicken and remove excess fat.
2. Place the chicken, Chinese yam, goji berries, red dates, ginger slices, and rice wine into a heatproof ceramic bowl.
3. Add enough water to cover the ingredients and seal with cling wrap.
4. Add water in a steamer and bring water to a boil. Place the bowl in the steamer.
5. Steam for 1½–2 hours with medium heat.
6. Remove from the steamer and season with salt.

Black chicken (silkie chicken) is also known as black-boned chicken, because its beak, bones, flesh, and skin are black or dark blue. It has a long tradition as a medicinal food. Modern research has found that silkie chickens contain a higher level of protein, vitamin B, 18 amino acids, and minerals, while its saturated fats and cholesterol are much lower. Black chicken is almost always cooked with herbs to alleviate certain ailments such as fatigue, osteoporosis, and iron-deficient anemia.

Chinese red dates, commonly known as jujubes outside of China, are regarded as both a fruit/spice and herb. It has long been heralded as a superfood, often prescribed by traditional Chinese-medicine doctors and appear frequently in locals' kitchens, where they're used to decorate buns, porridge, soup, or desserts as a kind of spice. You can get them fresh during the autumn, when they're crisp and green as apples, or dried, when the fruit takes on a deep-red color and sweet, chewy texture. Dried red dates can be found in most Asian grocery stores.

Chicken with Goji Berries and Red Dates

Ingredients

8½ cups hot water
1 silkie chicken or small organic chicken, rinsed clean, excess fat trimmed off, and cut into small pieces
10 dried red dates

1 tablespoon goji berries (wolf-berries)
Pinch salt

Directions

1. Boil 2 cups of water in a saucepan. Add chicken pieces, cook for 2 minutes (parboil), and drain.
2. Place the chicken into a pot (clay pot is preferred). Add remaining hot water.
3. Simmer for 1½ hours. Add dates and goji berries. Let simmer for another hour.
4. Add a bit of salt. Serve with both soup and meat.

This is a lighter version of Chicken with Goji Berries and Chinese Yam on page 206, loved by women for its nourishing nature. It's a common recipe for women suffering from fatigue, anemia, and menstrual pain.

One of the central principles of Chinese medicine is qi, the concept that the body is composed of different energy levels that must be perfectly balanced. Illness is thought to be caused by imbalances in qi. The role of blood is similar to qi, and also plays an important role in Chinese medicine. Many health conditions are thought to be the result of a fall in blood production. Traditional Chinese medicine states that this lack of blood production is due to a decrease in qi. A blood tonic may be recommended in order to stimulate increased blood production and qi.

Fish Soup with Tofu and Enoki Mushrooms

Ingredients

6 ounces saltwater fish fillet
½ teaspoon salt
1 teaspoon cooking wine
1 egg white, lightly beaten
¼ teaspoon pepper
½ tablespoon cooking oil
3 slices fresh ginger
2 cups chicken stock
2 cups water
3 ounces enoki mushrooms or oyster mushrooms

5 ounces silken (soft) tofu, cut into small cubes
4 pieces tender Shanghai bok choy leafs or Chinese Napa cabbage leafs
2 tablespoons cornstarch, mixed well with 4 tablespoons water
1 tablespoon green onion (scallions), chopped

Directions

1. Clean and marinate the fish with a mixture consisting of ½ teaspoon of salt, 1 teaspoon of cooking wine, egg white, and ¼ teaspoon of pepper.
2. Heat cooking oil in a saucepan or pot.
3. Add ginger slices to stir-fry for 30 seconds.
4. Add chicken stock and water, and bring to a boil.
5. Add salt, mushrooms, and fish. Cook for 10 minutes.
6. Add tofu, cooking for 3–5 minutes, and then add bok choy leafs.
7. Add cornstarch mixture, stir, and mix well.
8. Garnish with chopped green onion and serve.

Fish is one of the healthiest foods in the modern diet. It is high in protein and important vitamins, while being low in fat. Making soups with fish can be delicious, but the fish must be very fresh. Saltwater fish such as garoupa, red snapper, or threadfin are good for this recipe.

Beef Soup with Vegetables

Ingredients

10 ounces beef shin, cut into cubes

1½ tablespoons cooking oil

2 medium-size tomatoes, cut into small pieces

8½ liters water

½ cup tomato juice

3 teaspoons cooking wine

3 slices fresh ginger, sliced

1 onion, cut into small pieces

3 carrots, peeled and cut into cubes

5 potatoes, peeled and cut into cubes

1 stalk celery, cut into small pieces

½ teaspoon pepper

Salt, to taste

Directions

1. Parboil the beef for 2 minutes and drain.

2. In a saucepan, add cooking oil and heat until hot. Add tomato pieces and cook for 3–5 minutes or until juicy.

3. In a large pot, add water and bring to a boil.

4. Add tomato juice and beef, cooking wine, and ginger slices. Bring back to boil again, and then turn heat down to simmer for 1 hour.

5. Add onion, carrots, potatoes, and salt. Simmer for another 30–45 minutes.

6. Add celery, cooking for 20 minutes.

7. Garnish with pepper.

Beef is high in protein. Beef also contains many different types of amino acids, which are good for building and strengthening immunities, promoting healthy growth, and aiding recuperation. Beef suitable for consumption is particularly good as a stew or simmered soup, especially in the winter. People who are prone to illness or fatigue, especially those who have just recovered from a major illness or who are suffering from anemia, will benefit from consuming beef. However, for normal, healthy people, beef should be consumed in moderation.

Tough beef cuts like brisket, chuck, flank, shank, or shin are ideal for making Chinese beef soups, which often require long hours of simmering.

Oxtail Soup with Vegetables

Ingredients

8½ cups water
4 ginger slices
1 tablespoon cooking wine
1 pound sectioned oxtail bones, washed and soaked in water
2 teaspoons cooking oil
2 tomatoes, cut into small pieces

½ cup tomato juice
2 carrots, peeled and cut into sections
3 potatoes, peeled and cut into small pieces
2 teaspoons salt
1 teaspoon pepper

Directions

1. Bring water in a saucepan to a boil. Add half the ginger slices, cooking wine, and oxtail pieces. Cook for about 8–10 minutes.
2. Remove oxtail. Rinse with cold water and drain.
3. Bring 8½ cups of water in a large soup pot to a boil. Add remaining ginger slices and oxtail.
4. Lower the heat and simmer for 1 hour.
5. Heat a saucepan. Add cooking oil. Add tomato pieces, cooking until juicy.
6. Add tomato juice, carrot, and potato pieces to the soup pot. Cover and simmer for another 45 minutes.
7. Add salt and pepper to season.

This is a hearty, filling soup using nutritious root vegetables. If tomatoes are too dry when cooking, add a small amount of water and cook under low heat.

Lamb with Ginseng Porridge

Ingredients

½ pound lamb fillet, cut into smaller pieces
1 cup rice
6 cups water
2 ounces ginseng root
4 slices fresh ginger

2 teaspoons goji berries (wolfberries)
20 dried red dates
Pinch salt and white pepper powder or black pepper powder

Directions

1. Parboil the lamb pieces.
2. Rinse and soak the rice for 30 minutes.
3. Boil the water in a large pot or saucepan.
4. Add lamb, ginseng, and ginger.
5. Simmer on low-medium heat for 1 hour.
6. Add rice and simmer for 30 minutes.
7. Add goji berries and red dates. Simmer for another 30 minutes.
8. Add salt and pepper powder before serving.

This lamb fillet can be made from the cheaper lamb cuts. Leftover lamb is also perfect for this recipe. In this case, just dice or shred the leftover lamb meat into small pieces. Cook the rice first, and then add lamb pieces when the rice porridge is almost done (add with red dates and goji berries together).

This porridge can also be cooked with a slow cooker. This is a warming and comforting porridge for a new mother.

Mung Bean-Rice Porridge

Ingredients

½ cup mung beans
½ cup white rice
¼ cup brown rice
8½ cups water

Directions

1. Rinse mung beans and rice.
2. Add water to a large pot or saucepan.
3. Bring water to a boil; put all ingredients into the pot.
4. Bring to a boil again. Stir well, and then turn heat to low-medium until ingredients are sticky and softened. Stir occasionally to avoid sticking on the bottom.

Mung bean sprouts contain rich quantities of vitamins A, B, C, and E. They are also known to be an excellent source of many minerals, such as calcium, iron, and potassium. The bean is popular as an ideal food for weight-loss. It is recommended as a food supplement in many dieting programs, due to its very low fat content. It is a rich source of protein and fiber, which helps to reduce high cholesterol levels in the blood system.

The high fiber content of mung beans also includes complex carbohydrates, which aid digestion. Complex carbohydrates are also effective in stabilizing blood sugar and prevent rapid increases of blood sugar after meals. It also helps to keep the body's energy at a balanced level. Those who suffer from diabetes or high cholesterol will benefit from frequent consumption of mung beans.

In Chinese medicine, mung bean sprouts are considered a "cooling food," containing anticancer properties. Herbalists use them for all inflammatory conditions, ranging from systematic infections to heat stroke and even hypertension.

Rock sugar, also called crystal sugar, can be used in this recipe to make a nice summer dessert. You can find rock sugar in many Asian grocery stores—or simply replace it with regular sugar.

Lotus Seeds with Lily Bulbs

Ingredients

¼ dried lily bulb
20 red dates
½ cup lotus seeds
4¼ cups water
1 Chinese yam or any yam, peeled and cut into small pieces
⅓ cup rock sugar or regular sugar, to taste

Directions

1. Rinse lily bulb, red dates, and lotus seeds. Soak in water for an hour.
2. Add water in a soup pot. Add lily bulb and lotus seeds into the pot.
3. Bring water to a boil, turn heat to low, and simmer for 30 minutes.
4. Add red dates and Chinese yam; continue to simmer until yam and dates are soft.
5. Add rock sugar. Stir to dissolve.
6. To serve cold, put into the refrigerator until cool.

During hot summers, Chinese people will drink "sweet soups" like this one to help cool down, as well as to clean and refresh the body. This is a light and refreshing soup. As with most Chinese congee, these soups are mostly simmered for a fairly long time for flavor, and they can be served both hot and cold.

Lotus seeds or lotus nuts are the seeds of plants in the genus Nelumbo, particularly the species *Nelumbo nucifera*. The seeds are of great importance to east Asian cuisine and are used extensively in traditional Chinese medicine and in Chinese soups or desserts. They are most commonly sold in the shelled and dried form. When cooked in clear soups, lotus seeds are believed to "clear heat" and be particularly nutritious and restorative to one's health, which may explain the prevalence of their use in Chinese medicine.

Other ingredients that are considered "cooling" or restorative in Chinese medicines, which are often cooked in a sweetened soup with lotus seeds, include red beans (adzuki beans), red dates, mung beans, Job's tears, and cloud fungus (snow fungus).

Eight-Treasures Congee

Ingredients

12 cups water

⅓ cup red beans

⅓ cup kidney beans

⅓ cup black rice (optional: white rice)

⅓ cup sweet rice (sticky rice)

⅓ cup brown rice

⅓ cup millet

⅓ cup wheat

⅓ cup barley

⅓ cup shelled peanuts

½ cup dried longan fruit flesh or raisins

20–30 pitted dried red dates

½ cup sugar, or to taste

Directions

1. Rinse and drain all ingredients.

2. Use a large pot (a large stockpot is ideal), add water, and bring water to a boil. Add all ingredients (except longan, dates, and sugar) and cover. Keep to a simmer on low-medium heat for 3 hours or until thick and smooth.

3. Rinse dried longan fruit flesh and red dates, stirring both into the porridge together.

4. Cook for another hour.

5. Add sugar and stir well. Remove from stove and serve.

This congee (also known as ba bao zhou) is used in traditional Chinese medicine as a fast or cleanse. When cooking, stir occasionally to avoid sticking on the bottom. Add more water if necessary. If you want to form a sticky and smooth congee more quickly, add ½ cup of oatmeal.

This recipe is very flexible; you can use more than eight ingredients or fewer. Many candied fruits like grapefruit peel, kumquats, orange and lemon rinds, fresh cherries, and pineapple are all suitable for this recipe.

Laba Congee

Ingredients

10–12 cups water
⅓ cup rice
⅓ cup millet
⅓ cup sticky yellow rice
⅓ cup sweet rice (sticky rice)
⅓ cup red beans
⅓ cup dried longan or raisins

⅓ cup dried red dates , or any candied fruit like grapefruit peel, orange and lemon rinds, fresh cherries, or pineapple
⅓ cup chestnuts
⅓ cup lotus seeds (optional)
⅓ cup shelled peanuts
⅓ cup oatmeal
Sugar, to taste

Directions

1. Rinse and drain all ingredients.
2. Use a large pot (a large stockpot is ideal), add water, and bring to a boil. Add rice, millet, sticky yellow rice, sticky rice, and red beans, and cover. Keep to a simmer on low-medium heat for 3 hours or until thick and smooth. Stir occasionally to avoid sticking on the bottom.
3. Rinse dried longan fruit flesh, red dates, chestnuts, lotus seeds, shelled peanuts, and oatmeal. Stir into the porridge.
4. Cook for another hour.
5. Add sugar and stir well. Remove from stove and serve.

This is a variation of Eight-Treasures Congee on page 220, which is a healthy multigrain rice porridge. This Laba congee is a ceremonial dish eaten on the 8th day of the 12th month in the Chinese calendar to celebrate the harvest. The earliest rice porridge was prepared using red beans, but it has now developed into many different kinds. It was mainly made up of many kinds of rice, beans, dried fruit, nuts or even potato, meat, and vegetables. This is a healthy food for winter.

Mushroom-Rice Porridge

Ingredients

1 ounce dried black wood-ear mushrooms

10 dried Chinese shiitake mushrooms

6 cups water or vegetarian soup stock

1 carrot

2 ounces bamboo shoots

15 pieces dried straw mushrooms

2 cups white rice

½ cup oatmeal

Pinch salt

Dash pepper

Dash cooking oil

Dash sesame seed oil

Directions

1. Soak the black wood-ear mushrooms and shiitake mushrooms in lukewarm water for 30 minutes or until softened. Rinse clean.
2. Clean and dice the carrot.
3. Clean and dice the bamboo shoot.
4. Parboil the black wood-ear mushrooms and straw mushrooms.
5. Bring the water to a boil, add rice, and cook for 1 hour.
6. Add oatmeal and cook for 15 minutes.
7. Add the straw mushrooms, carrot, bamboo shoot, and black wood-ear mushrooms. Cook for 10 minutes.
8. Add the seasonings, sprinkle cooking oil and sesame seed oil on top, and serve.

Desserts

Coconut Balls

Ingredients

½ cup coconut flakes, or as needed

1½ cups sweet-rice flour (sticky-rice flour)

¼ cup sweetened condensed milk

⅓–½ cup boiling water, or as needed

5 tablespoons sweet red-bean paste, or as needed

2–3 tablespoons sugar (optional)

Directions

1. Spread the coconut flakes on a baking sheet and set aside.
2. Place the sweet-rice flour in a large mixing bowl. Slowly add the sweetened condensed milk, using a spoon to stir it into the flour.
3. Slowly add the boiled water, using the spoon to stir it in. Knead the flour for at least 1 minute (more kneading creates a chewier texture). Then add more boiling water, 1 tablespoon or less at a time, working and shaping the dough until it has a texture similar to dough—not too soft, but easy to manipulate.
4. Roll the dough into a 10-inch log.
5. To fill the coconut balls: Cut off a 1-inch piece of dough. (Cover the remainder of the dough with a damp towel or wrap in plastic wrap to keep it from drying out while you are preparing the coconut balls.) Roll into a ball, and then flatten with the palm of your hand so you have a 2–2½-inch circle. Place about 1½ teaspoons red-bean paste into the center and gently fold the dough over.
6. Gently squeeze the dough and form back into a ball, rolling with your hands. Continue with the remainder of the dough.

7. Place the coconut balls in the boiling water. Use spoon or a turner to move the balls occasionally to avoid sticking to the bottom. Cook on medium-high heat until the balls rise and are floating on the top (about 6–7 minutes).

8. Roll the balls in the coconut. Eat the coconut balls the same day.

This kind of sticky ball (usually prepared without a coconut coating) is called tang yuan in China, a sweet dumpling served as a popular snack during the Spring Festival and the Lantern Festival. The round shape is a symbol for family reunion and a wish for a peaceful and safe New Year.

This recipe makes 10 coconut rice balls and can easily be doubled to make 20. Red-bean paste makes a nice filling because it is quite malleable; however, feel free to experiment with other fillings if desired—a combination of crushed peanuts and brown sugar, sesame-seed paste with sugar, or a mixture of softened butter, coconut, and sugar would be good choices.

Sweet-rice flour (also known as sticky-rice flour) can be a bit tricky to work with—at first, it looks too dry, and the next thing you know, the dough is sticking to your hands because you've added too much water. If that happens, add a bit more sweet-rice flour. On the other hand, if the dough is too dry, add more boiled water, a small amount at a time.

Baked Chinese New Year Cake

Ingredients

1 (16-ounce) bag sweet-rice flour (sticky-rice flour)
½ cup vegetable or olive oil
3 eggs
2 cups milk
1–1¾ cups sugar, to taste

1 teaspoon baking powder
1 teaspoon vanilla extract
1 can red adzuki beans or 1 cup raisins
Cooking spray

Directions

1. Mix everything but the beans in a large bowl. Mix and stir well.
2. Grease a 9– by 13-inch baking dish (or spray with nonstick cooking spray).
3. Spread half of the batter into the baking dish.
4. Spread the beans or raisins evenly over the batter.
5. Spread the other half of the batter over the beans.
6. Bake in oven at 350°F for 40–50 minutes.
7. Test for doneness by using a chopstick; if it comes out clean, it is done.
8. Cut into squares after cooling down.

This sweet version of Baked Chinese New Year Cake (also known as nian gao) has a slightly sticky texture.

While traditional nian gao is steamed and does not contain oil, eggs, or other ingredients normally found in a cake batter, this baking version is very easy to make.

If fat is a concern, use less oil. Sweetened red-bean paste is also a good alternative; in that case, use less sugar in the batter.

It will turn hard after a day; microwave for 30 seconds for one piece and it will turn soft again.

Almond Float

Ingredients

1 packet unflavored gelatin
4 tablespoons granulated sugar
1 cup boiling water
2 teaspoons almond extract, as desired
1 cup evaporated milk

1 cup cold water
1 can fruit cocktail with syrup

Directions

1. In a medium bowl, combine the gelatin and the sugar, stirring to mix well.
2. Pour the boiling water over the gelatin-sugar mixture and stir until completely dissolved.
3. Stir in the almond extract, evaporated milk, and the cold water, mixing well.
4. Pour the gelatin into a bowl or serving mold if desired. Chill until firm.
5. To serve, cut the gelatin into 1-inch squares or diamonds and serve with the canned fruit and syrup from the can. The almond float may be prepared in advance and refrigerated (not frozen) until ready to serve.

Almond floats are a refreshing dessert that can be served with canned or fresh fruit. This recipe is very adaptable, so feel free to use various types of canned or fresh fruit.
   You can substitute almond with lemon or vanilla extract. Use canned mandarin oranges or other canned fruit in place of the fruit cocktail.

Eight-Precious Pudding

Ingredients

2 tablespoons lotus seeds
2 cups cold water
10 dried Chinese red dates
2 cups sweet rice (sticky rice)
¼ cup sugar
3 tablespoons oil

1 red maraschino cherry, stem removed
1 cup any candied fruits
1 cup red-bean paste

Directions

1. Add lotus seeds to cold water in a saucepan. Bring to a boil. Simmer on low heat for 20 minutes. Drain and cool. Split into halves. Set aside.

2. Soak red dates in warm water for 30 minutes. Set aside.

3. Put rice in a rice cooker with water level ¾ inch above rice (or follow rice cooking instructions). When it's done, stir in sugar and oil. Mix well. Set aside.

4. Grease medium-size bowl well with oil. Place cherry in center. Arrange lotus seeds, red dates, and candied fruits in circles around the bottom and up to the edge of the bowl, glazed-side down.

5. Spread a layer of rice mixture in the bowl, then spooning a layer of red-bean paste over the rice. Spread with another layer of rice. Be careful not to spoil the design. Pack tightly.

6. Place the bowl in steamer. Steam for 1 hour. Remove pudding carefully by using a spatula around the edge. Put a serving plate over the bowl and invert.

Serve pudding with Sweet Almond Sauce: Boil 3 tablespoons of sugar in 1 cup of water, stirring to dissolve the sugar. Stir in 1 teaspoon of almond extract. Thicken with 1 tablespoon of cornstarch dissolved in 2 tablespoons of water.

While Westerners traditionally end their evening meal with a fancy dessert, the Chinese prefer to eat fruit (a much healthier custom). Desserts do not feature prominently in Chinese cooking. Still, a few Chinese desserts have caught on in the West. A well-known treat—normally reserved for special occasions—is Eight-Precious Pudding (it may also be called "Eight-Treasure pudding" or "Eight-Precious Rice"). This rice pudding is filled with an assortment of colorful fruits such as maraschino cherries and dates, each representing a "treasure"—a precious stone such as ruby or jade.

This recipe is very flexible; you can use more than eight ingredients or fewer. Many candied fruits like grapefruit peel, kumquats, orange and lemon rinds, fresh cherries, and pineapple are all suitable for this recipe.

Chilled Fruit Salad

Ingredients

1 cup water

4 ounces rock sugar or 6 table-spoons granulated sugar

2 tablespoons mango juice (fresh or canned)

1 cup mango slices (fresh or canned)

1 cup sliced papaya

1 peach or apple, sliced

2 kiwi fruit, stems cut off, pared, and cut into thin slices

1 tangerine, peeled and separated into individual segments

4–8 lychees or pineapple pieces or fresh strawberries (optional)

Directions

1. Bring the water, rock sugar, and mango juice to a boil over medium-low heat, stirring to dissolve the rock sugar. Cool.

2. Toss all of the fruit with the sugar-syrup mixture. Spoon 1–1¼ cups into each dessert serving plate (can make 4 servings). Chill until ready to serve.

Variation: Chilled-Melon Fruit Salad

Using hollowed-out honeydew melon halves to serve this colorful and healthy fruit salad is even more appealing. If you're preparing your own melon halves from whole honeydew melons, feel free to substitute the scooped-out honeydew for the papaya, mango, or peach as desired.

Rock sugar is a popular ingredient in Chinese desserts. It can be found at Asian markets, or you can substitute with 6 tablespoons of granulated sugar.

Feel free to use whatever fresh fruits are in season for the filling, or other melons such as cantaloupe for the "bowl." If fresh mango is unavailable, substitute canned mango slices and juice.

Red-Bean Cake

Ingredients

1 cup red beans
6 cups water
¼ cup granulated sugar
1 cup coconut milk
½ cup skim milk
Few threads of agar

Directions

1. Clean red beans. Add red beans and water in a cooker. Cook for 2 hours or until red beans break up.
2. Add crystal sugar, coconut milk, and milk. Bring to a boil. Turn off heat, setting aside.
3. Add a cup of water in a saucepan, and add agar. Stir constantly until agar melts.
4. Add red-bean mixture (you don't need to pour all the mixture in if it is too much) and stir evenly.
5. Turn off the heat. Pour the mixture in a deep plate. It will become solid after 30 minutes at room temperature.
6. Cut into the desired shape and arrange on a plate.

(see note on next page)

Red-bean desserts are very popular in Chinese cuisine. They are widely used in porridges, cakes, and soups. Red-bean paste is used in all kinds of desserts, the most popular of which is stuffed into a bun.

Eating red-bean desserts helps to clear away heat and toxins, as well as remove body fluids, so it is often included in weight-loss plans

Ready-to-use bean pastes are available in many Asian supermarkets, but they usually contain lots of sugar. However, it's not too difficult to make it yourself, so you can add less sugar and prepare truly healthy desserts.

Acknowledgments

Special thanks to a team of translators made of college students who have provided great assistance during this publishing process. Without their diligent work, it would be tough for us to transcend the real Chinese flavors and dietary health in this book.

These young students are: Lingyi Sun, Xiaoye Wang, Audrey Zhang Yang, Chunan Liu, Xingzhe He, Jun Xu, Sue Xu, Shijing Zhang, Xiangxuan Kong, Congwen Wang, Jing Zhu, Hong Zhu, Feifei Zhang, Rui Zhang, and Janet Shuai Gao.

About the Authors

Jo Brielyn is the co-author of *Combat Fat for Kids: The Complete Plan for Family Fitness, Nutrition, and Health*. She is also a contributing writer for Hatherleigh Press and has currently completed 14 other nonfiction books about health and wellness.

Wang Renxiang is an eminent archaeologist in China. One of his major research areas has been on the dietetic culture from the perspective of archaeology. He has published many books in Chinese on the subjects of gourmet food, cooking, and culture.

David W. Wang is a senior consultant of international business and cross-cultural communications based in Washington, D.C. He is the author of the recent worldwide best-selling book, *Decoding the Dragon's Mindset*.